FDR *on* DEMOCRACY

FDR *on* DEMOCRACY

THE GREATEST SPEECHES AND WRITINGS OF PRESIDENT FRANKLIN DELANO ROOSEVELT

Selected and Introduced by
HARVEY J. KAYE

Skyhorse Publishing

Skyhorse Publishing books may be purchased in bulk at special discounts for sales promotion, corporate gifts, fund-raising, or educational purposes. Special editions can also be created to specifications. For details, contact the Special Sales Department, Skyhorse Publishing, 307 West 36th Street, 11th Floor, New York, NY 10018 or info@skyhorsepublishing.com.

Skyhorse® and Skyhorse Publishing® are registered trademarks of Skyhorse Publishing, Inc.®, a Delaware corporation.

Visit our website at www.skyhorsepublishing.com.

10 9 8 7 6 5 4 3 2 1

Library of Congress Cataloging-in-Publication Data is available on file.

Cover design by Brian Peterson
Cover photo by Getty Images

ISBN: 978-1-5107-5216-0
Ebook ISBN: 978-1-5107-5217-7

Printed in the United States of America

Dedicated to my friends
at the FDR Presidential Library and Museum
Paul Sparrow, Cliff Laube, Sal Assenza, Steve Lomazow,
and Bill vanden Heuvel

Contents

Introduction

"Democracy is not a static thing. It is an everlasting march."
—**Franklin Roosevelt, October 1, 1935**

We Americans rightly remember and honor Franklin Delano Roosevelt for his presidential leadership. Indeed, when historians and pollsters ask us to rank the nation's presidents, we consistently rate him, alongside George Washington and Abraham Lincoln, as one of our three greatest. How could we not? In the course of his twelve-year presidency, from 1933 to 1945, FDR rallied Americans to stand forth, confront, and ultimately triumph over the two worst crises to threaten the United States in the twentieth century: the Great Depression and the Second World War. These were mortal crises that placed the very survival of the United States, and all that it stood for, in jeopardy. And yet, as much as we have honored and memorialized Roosevelt and his presidency by naming parks and schools after him and by erecting monuments to him—the grandest in Washington, DC, and New York City—we regularly forget, or are made to forget, what made him a truly great leader. But in the wake of more than forty years of assaults on the memory and legacy of Roosevelt from the right and the corporate rich, and especially now, in light of the crises we ourselves face, we need to start remembering.

We need to remember not only that Franklin Roosevelt successfully mobilized Americans to rescue the United States from economic ruin in the 1930s; to save the nation and the world from Nazi, fascist, and imperial tyranny in the first half of the 1940s; *and* to build an America that at war's end would become the strongest and most prosperous country on earth. We need to also remember that he did so—against fierce conservative and reactionary opposition, despite Americans' own many faults and failings, and in spite of his own elite background and physical disabilities—by inspiring, encouraging, and empowering his fellow citizens, especially working Americans, to make the United States freer, more equal, and more democratic than ever before. In fact, we need to remember that he and the generation he led actually lifted the nation out of the Depression, defended it against its fascist enemies in a global war, and actually made it even stronger and greater: not by retreating from what it meant to be an American, but by radically extending and deepening American democratic life.

In this collection of Roosevelt's speeches and writings, we encounter the words—words such as "The only thing we have to fear is fear itself" and "This generation of Americans has a rendezvous with destiny"—that helped to turn a generation of American men and women into what we have come to recognize as our "Greatest Generation" and, in turn, led them to consider him their greatest leader. Words that in the face of terrible and devastating catastrophes reminded them who they were and what they were capable of accomplishing. Words that not only recruited them to and enlisted them in the labors and struggles of the New Deal and World War II, but also invited them to organize and press him to advance industrial democracy and social democracy even further than he himself might ever have originally intended to go. Words that emboldened a generation to progressively transform themselves and the nation.

From the 1920s through the New Deal 1930s and World War II, FDR advanced a vision of America's future rooted in the nation's historic promise and the democratic history it engendered. He did so in his Commonwealth Club speech of 1932, when he called for a new "economic declaration of rights"; in his 1941 Annual Message to Congress, when he pronounced the "four freedoms" to be "Freedom of Speech and Expression, Freedom of Worship, Freedom from Want, Freedom from Fear"; and in his 1944 State of the Union address, when he projected the enactment of a second Bill of Rights, an Economic Bill of Rights for all Americans (all of which are included in this volume).

Yes, the words were written and spoken decades ago. Nonetheless, despite the best efforts of powerful and richly endowed forces to make them seem strange or foreign to our eyes and ears, we not only recognize many of them, but also hear them speaking directly to us, to our persistent democratic hopes and aspirations—imbued in or afforded us by his presidency and the generation that elected him president four times.

WHO WAS FDR? What made him a champion of American democratic life—a champion determined to not simply rhetorically celebrate the United States but, all the more, to encourage his fellow citizens to truly enhance it?

Born in 1882, Franklin Roosevelt grew up privileged, the son of New York Hudson River gentry. But whereas his older cousin President Theodore Roosevelt, whom he greatly admired and often sought to model himself after, was a Republican-turned-Progressive, FDR was a Democrat who began his career as a Progressive but moved beyond progressivism to develop a new kind of liberalism and to become, rather amazingly, a small-*d* democrat.

Privilege led young Franklin to private school, then on to Harvard, and finally into Columbia University Law School. Along the way, to his extremely good fortune, he met, fell in love with, and married his cousin Eleanor, Theodore's niece, who would be his invaluable political partner for the rest of his life and become, in the course of the 1930s, the most prominent woman in America and, eventually, the world.

After his studies, ambition soon propelled FDR into politics. He won a challenging election to the New York state legislature in 1910 and two years later moved from Albany to Washington to serve in President Woodrow Wilson's cabinet as Assistant Secretary of the Navy, a post that, with the onset of World War I in 1914 and US entry into the war in 1917, afforded him experiences and skills that would come in handy years later as a wartime president.

Privilege, prominence, and personal determination propelled FDR forward. But they could not save him from terrible defeats and setbacks. To his credit and our advantage, he would not retreat in the face of crises.

In 1920, he succeeded in securing the second slot on the ill-fated Democratic Party presidential ticket. The Democrats lost the election that year in good part because the Republicans effectively portrayed President Wilson's plan for the postwar League of Nations, and possible United States membership in it, as a threat to American sovereignty. FDR himself had strongly supported American membership as a means of maintaining peace in the world, and he would never actually give up the idea of the United States participating in such a global institution—which led him during World War II to envision, propose, and pursue the creation of the United Nations.

Out of office and government following the 1920 defeat, Roosevelt set himself—inspired by the authorial examples of his presidential "mentors" Theodore Roosevelt and Woodrow Wilson—to try writing a new history of the United States. As he put it, he was not impressed with existing texts. They failed to show, he said, that the United States was "clearly going somewhere right from the start." However, he soon discovered that while he was good with words, he was not a book-writing man. But in his own way he actually would "write" a new American story. Winning the presidency in 1932, FDR would become not just Commander in Chief, but also, as the speeches collected here attest, "History Teacher in Chief." The history—the historical narrative—he would cultivate in his speeches was that of a nation made great and democratic by the progressive, at times radical, impulses and energies of its people.

Of course, the most devastating and tragic setback that Roosevelt would suffer and endure came in 1921, when he contracted polio at the age of thirty-nine. Thereafter, as much as he struggled to find a cure and a way of overcoming the paralysis in his legs caused by the disease, he would never again stand up or walk without assistance. And yet, testifying to both the extraordinary aid and support of his family and friends and his own determination not to surrender to the disease, he would become by decade's end the most dynamic political figure in the country.

All through the 1920s, FDR worked hard to transcend his disability. He would never find a cure, but the experience taught him more than to appreciate how interdependent we are upon one another to survive and move ahead. It also made him more sympathetic for and empathetic toward those in need. At the same time, he was learning about the economic difficulties and struggles of working people, courtesy of Eleanor, who had become deeply involved in the Women's Trade Union League in New York City and regularly brought many a working-class labor and socialist activist home to the family estate at Hyde Park. These women, mostly East European Jewish immigrants, were helping to turn him all the more into a small-*d* democrat and to prepare him to become the leader he soon became.

Notably, the leftist writer and editor Max Lerner would observe in a 1938 essay titled "Roosevelt and History" that FDR "will be remembered . . . as a man who, without being of the people . . . was able to grasp and to some degree communicate what the common man dimly felt."

And as Lerner and others were to note, what made that possible was that Roosevelt himself was "wholeheartedly a democrat" who sincerely wanted to know what Americans were truly thinking. Moreover, people close to him would say that despite his elite background, he imagined his fellow citizens possessing the same democratic memories, impulses, and longings as he did.

REPUBLICANS GOVERNED IN Washington for twelve years, but their political ascendance would be undone by the devastating financial crash of 1929 and the ensuing depression and economic and social catastrophes— factory and bank closures, skyrocketing unemployment, widespread loss of homes and homesteads, widening and deepening poverty and destitution, and vast numbers of people, children included, living in Hoovervilles (shantytowns named after Republican president Herbert Hoover) or traveling the roads and rails.

In the face of such horrors, more and more Americans feared for the future. Some yearned for a dictator. Others, from industrial workers to midwestern farmers, began to organize demonstrations, marches, and mass protests. In the midst of this Roosevelt remarked to a friend, "There is no question in my mind that it is time for the country to become fairly radical for at least one generation." Only in this way, he thought, could the United States avoid a fascist or communist revolution and sustain its own historic and persistent *democratic* revolution.

UNWILLING TO REMAIN sidelined, Roosevelt had reentered politics in 1928 and won two consecutive two-year terms as governor of New York. As governor, he responded to the crash and worsening depression by using the powers of state government to address the economic and social crises. Rejecting the traditional ideal of limited government, he launched public works projects and initiatives to create jobs for the unemployed. His initiatives in New York made him a prime candidate for president.

Convinced that President Herbert Hoover and his conservative Republican administration were contributing to the ruination of the country, FDR declared for the presidency in 1932, intent upon leading the United States out of the Great Depression by leading it in a liberal, progressive, indeed one might actually say *social-democratic* direction. Promising a New Deal of federal policies and programs that would not only provide economic relief, instigate economic recovery, and undertake the reconstruction of the nation, thereby creating jobs and affording economic security to the "forgotten man" (that is, to working people), but also empower Americans to democratically reform government and public life, he would handily defeat the incumbent Hoover that November.

Conservatives and corporate bosses rightly worried about Roosevelt's plans and initiatives, and they would soon organize well-funded media campaigns to undo his presidency by portraying the president as a communist or a socialist and a threat to American liberty. But he was neither. He did not envision nationalizing banks, industries, and agriculture. He did, however, firmly believe, as had his forerunner Abraham Lincoln, that democratic government existed to do what we could not do for ourselves—or what high finance and big business were either failing to do or doing wrongly or unjustly. Moreover, he and his cabinet officers were not seeking to weaken or undermine the Bill of Rights, but to strengthen it by extending its reach and empowering citizens and workers against the power and authority of corporate property and wealth.

Declaring at his first inauguration in 1933 that "the only thing we have to fear is fear itself," Roosevelt now set himself, his "New Dealers," and the Democratic-controlled Congress to mobilizing Americans to the labors and struggles of relief, recovery, reconstruction, and reform. Together, president and people would severely test each other, make mistakes and regrettable compromises, and suffer defeats and disappointments. Nevertheless, challenging each other to live up to their finest ideals, Roosevelt and his fellow citizens would advance them further than either had expected or even imagined possible. We should not fail to note that FDR was to win an historic landslide vote in the November 1936 presidential election.

Confronting fierce conservative, reactionary, and corporate opposition, Roosevelt and the American people not only utterly rejected authoritarianism, but also enthusiastically redeemed the nation's historic purpose and promise by initiating revolutionary changes in American government and public life and radically extending American freedom, equality, and democracy. Harnessing the powers of democratic government, they subjected big business and finance to public account and regulation; empowered the federal government to address the needs of working people; mobilized and organized labor unions; fought for their rights; broadened and leveled the "We" in "We the People"; established a social security system;

expanded the nation's public infrastructure; improved the environment; cultivated the arts and refashioned popular culture; and, while much remained to be done, imbued themselves with fresh democratic convictions, hopes, and aspirations that would enable them to go all out to victory in World War II.

In the wake of Imperial Japan's attack on Pearl Harbor, and the ensuing declarations of war by Japan's allies Nazi Germany and Fascist Italy, president and people would once again test each other, make mistakes and compromises, and suffer defeats and disappointments. Nonetheless, they not only prevailed over their enemies, but also, as before, compelled each other to enhance American democratic life in the process. Despite continuing antidemocratic opposition from the political right and conservative rich, Americans expanded the labor, consumer, and civil-rights movements; subjected industry and the marketplace to greater public control; began to dramatically reduce inequality and poverty; and further transformed the "We" in "We the People." Moreover, they embraced the prospect of new initiatives to expand freedom, equality, and democracy at war's end. And though FDR's declared hopes of enacting an Economic Bill of Rights that would guarantee such things as jobs, healthcare, housing, and education was obstructed by a coalition of Republicans and Southern Democrats, he did succeed in securing passage of the GI Bill—with major grassroots lobbying efforts by the American Legion—which enabled twelve million American veterans to remake themselves and the nation for the better in the postwar years.

Roosevelt passed away in April 1945. American citizens across the country and in uniform overseas mourned the loss of the man whom they had chosen four times not only to be their president, but also to challenge them to redeem, sustain, and advance America's purpose and promise. Germany and Japan would surrender in the months that followed (Italy had surrendered in 1943). But the generation that FDR inspired to greatness was just beginning to make America greater.

Roosevelt and the generation he led confronted mortal national and international crises and prevailed by making America "fairly radical for at least one generation." Neither he nor they were saints. FDR made terrible and tragic mistakes as president. He failed to get Congress to affirm America's historic commitment to serving as an "asylum for mankind" by lifting the nation's immigration and refugee quotas and enabling greater numbers of Jews to escape Hitler's Germany and find a safe haven in the United States. He allowed his generals and admirals to persuade him to create a "Jim Crow" racially segregated military to fight in World War II. And he deferred to the pressures and demands of powerful groups to remove Japanese Americans on the West Coast from their homes and farms and send them to internment in camps in the nation's interior. We must never, ever forget those things.

But neither should we fail to recall and appreciate, first, how FDR led Americans to victory in the darkest of times by encouraging them to progressively transform the nation and themselves and radically extend and deepen American democratic life, and second, how those very Americans who endured the anti-Semitism and racism that prevailed in this country at that time refused to allow the powers that be to get away with defining them as less American than any of their fellow citizens. They served no less patriotically and gallantly in the war effort and the fight against fascism and imperialism.

As we read the speeches and writings of FDR collected here, we would do well to keep in mind the words of his campaign advisor and cabinet officer, Rexford Tugwell. Early in *The Democratic Roosevelt*, his 1955 memoir and history of working with FDR, Tugwell offered this advice:

> We are a lucky people. We have had leaders when the national life was at stake. If it had not been for Washington we might not have become a nation; if it had not been for Lincoln we might have been split in two; if it had not been for this later democrat [Franklin Roosevelt] we might have succumbed to a dictatorship. For that was the alternative, much in the air, when he took charge. It is important that younger Americans who did not know him should understand what he found, what he left, and above all, how he went about his work. His attitudes and the devices he used are the ones called for among us. They will have to be improved and used again. Our troubles are not over; they will never be over. We must hope for other such leaders in other days of crisis. They can learn from studying the Roosevelt technique.

This historian would simply add that whether our parents and grandparents were lucky or just damn smart enough to choose the right leaders, they obviously recognized that Franklin Roosevelt himself was a fighter who would not just fight *for* them, but also encourage the fight *in* them. Inspired by his words and confidence, they defeated their enemies and made America stronger and richer by making it freer, more equal, and more democratic. If anybody was lucky, it was surely us.

But we need more than luck to confront our own crises. We must lay claim to Roosevelt's words and the struggles and achievements of the generation they shaped. And we should not fail to seriously consider FDR's advice to make America "fairly radical for at least a generation."

Suggested Readings

Elizabeth Borgwardt, *A New Deal for the World: America's Vision for Human Rights* (Harvard University Press, 2005).

Frank Freidel, *Franklin D. Roosevelt: A Rendezvous with Destiny* (Little, Brown and Company, 1990).

Harvey J. Kaye, *The Fight for the Four Freedoms: What Made FDR and the Greatest Generation Truly Great* (Simon & Schuster, 2014).

David M. Kennedy, *Freedom from Fear: The American People in Depression and War* (Oxford University Press, 1999).

PART I

New York State Senate and Governorship of New York
(1910–1932)

1.

We Have Acquired a New Set of Conditions Which We Must Seek to Solve

Speech to the People's Forum
Troy, New York, March 3, 1912

Roosevelt won election to the New York State Senate in 1910 as a Democrat and quickly became associated with the progressives of the party. However, he revealed his own political commitments by way of his legislative initiatives more than by way of any clearly stated philosophy. And yet, in this speech in the spring of 1912, we can hear him not only starting to articulate his democratic sense of history and progressive thinking, but also seeking to develop a new kind of American liberal—if not social-democratic—thinking, when he points to the emerging "new theory of the liberty of the community."

. . . . For nearly one thousand years and in almost every European and American country [the struggle to obtain individual freedom] has been the great and fundamental question in the economic life of the people. The Reformation, for instance, and the Renaissance in Europe are too commonly regarded as religious or educational struggles and have not, by teachers of history, been sufficiently explained as efforts on the part of the various peoples affected to obtain individual liberty. In the same way the American Revolution, the French Revolution and at a later date the general European uprisings of 1848. . . .

During the past century we have acquired a new set of conditions which we must seek to solve. To put it in the simplest and fewest words I have called this new theory the struggle for liberty of the community rather than liberty of the individual. When all is said and done every new doctrine which had been advanced for the last fifty years comes under this definition. Every new star that people have hitched their wagon to for the past half century, whether it be anti-rebating, or anti-trusts, or new-fashioned education, or conservation of our natural resources or state regulation of common carriers, or commission government, or any of the thousand and one other things that we have run after of late, almost without any exception come under the same heading. They are all steps in the evolution of the new theory of the liberty of the community.

The Socialist has at times called this same thing "community interest" and some sounding orators have called it the "brotherhood of man." Neither of these expressions is possible to use anywhere outside of heaven, for community of interest at once suggests to the mind a kind of happy condition where everybody wants the same thing and everybody gets it. This is comparatively recent doctrine, but at least the liberty of the individual has been obtained, and we must face new theories.

To state it plainly, competition has been shown to be useful up to a certain point, but co-operation, which is the thing that we must strive for today, begins where competition leaves off. This was what the founders of the Republic were groping for. . . .

So it is in New York State today. We are beginning to see that it is necessary for our health and happiness that the rights of individuals that lumber companies may not do as they please with the wooded growths in the Catskills and the Adirondacks.

There are, however, many persons who still think that individuals can do as they please with their own property even though it affects a community. The most striking example of what happens in such a case that I know of, was a picture shown me by Gifford Pinchot last week. It was a photograph of a walled city in northern China. Four or five hundred years ago this city had been the center of the populous and prosperous district, a district whose mountains and ridges were covered with magnificent trees, its streams flowing without interruption and its crops in the valleys prospering. It was known as one of the richest provinces in China, both as a lumber exporting center and as an agricultural community.

Today the picture shows the walled town, almost as it stood 500 years ago, but there is not a human being within the walls, and but few in the whole region. Rows upon rows of bare ridges and mountains stretch back from the city without a vestige of life. Everything is in a dilapidated condition, and this is all due to the liberty of the individual. This is what will happen in this very state if the individuals are allowed to do as they please with the natural resources to line their own pockets during their life. With them the motto is "After us the deluge." They do not care what happens after they are gone and even do not care what happens to their neighbors . . .

There is, to my mind, no valid reason why the food supply of the nation should not be put on the most economical and at the same time the most productive basis by carrying out co-operation. If we call the method regulation, people hold up their hands in horror and say "un-American," or "dangerous," but if we call the same identical process co-operation these same old fogies will cry out "well done." It may seem absurd to call the rebating formerly done by railroads, and the great trusts so-called, minor issues, but after all rebating was discrimination and the doctrine of co-operation came with it. The same with trusts; they were and are run on the theory of monopoly, but co-operations puts monopoly out of date and we now understand that the mere size of a trust is not of necessity its evil. The trust is evil because it monopolizes for a few, and as long as this keeps up it will be necessary for a community to change its features.

And here I come to the final point. How must the liberty of the community be obtained? It will not be obtained at once, whether the Democrats, Republicans, or Socialists say so or not. It must be worked out by keeping ever in view the cause of the condition and we must also keep in view the other essential point: law and order.

2.

Is There a Jefferson on the Horizon?

Review of Claude Bowers's *Jefferson and Hamilton*
New York Evening World, December 8, 1925

Out of political office in the early 1920s—following the defeat of the Democratic ticket on which he was the party's vice-presidential nominee— Roosevelt sought to write a book-length work of American history, just as his political idols Presidents Theodore Roosevelt and Woodrow Wilson had, but he ultimately failed to do so. In this book review essay, however, he not only reveals his democratic understanding of United States history and embraces the popular democratic legacy of Thomas Jefferson, he also essentially speaks of the kind of man he himself hopes to become and the kind of history he hopes to make as a politician.

I felt like saying "At last" as I read Mr. Claude G. Bowers's thrilling *Jefferson and Hamilton*. Perhaps this feeling is influenced by my personal experiences, but, in the broader sense, I am convinced that it would be a supreme contribution to current thought if the simple historic facts of this book could be learned in the newspaper editorial rooms as well as in the homes and schools of America.

Let me explain the personal side of it. A year ago I took occasion in a letter addressed to more than a thousand Democratic leaders throughout the country to refer in passing to the difference between the Jeffersonian and Hamiltonian ideals for an American method of government, and to apply their fundamental differences to present-day policies of our two great parties. Immediately many editors, including even some of the metropolitan press, launched sneers at the mere suggestion that Jeffersonianism could, in any remote manner, bear upon the America of 1925. A materialistic press reflects a materialistic age, but I still boil inwardly when I think of these smug writers who, wish being father to the thought, deny that the forces hostile to control of government by the people which existed in the crisis of 1790–1800 could still be a threat in our day and land.

The other personal reason is that for some years I have been, frankly, fed up with the romantic cult which has, since the publication of an historical novel, surrounded the name of Alexander Hamilton; and I have longed to write this very book, which now so much more ably comes from the delightful pen and untiring research of Mr. Bowers.

What is more valuable, however, is that in this study of a period which was, in every way, as important to the preservation of the Union as was the Civil War itself, a spirit of fairness and calm judgment is shown which makes the book not merely convincing to the general reader but of permanent value to the advanced student.

For Hamilton emerges still a romantic and fascinating figure, albeit in his true character of aristocrat and convinced opponent of popular government. And in Jefferson we see not only the savior of the deeper ideals of the Revolution, but also the man with human failings, the consummate politician.

The history of the United States may be interesting to some for the mere fact of events or personalities, but it is of value to us as a whole because of the application we make of these facts to present problems. It is in this spirit in which the book must be read: if we obtain from its pages only the knowledge of the definite establishment of a democratic republic because of the leadership of Jefferson and his associates, we fail unless we in addition apply the basic ideals of those days to the later events in American history and to the often essentially similar problems that still lie unsolved before us.

In fact what is the chief revelation is not the day by day contest of the first ten years of the constitutional United States, but the constantly recurring thought of parallel or at least analogous situations existing in our own generation.

Mr. Bowers's book enters into the midst of the organization of the government in 1789 after the ratification of the Constitution and the election of President Washington . . . There were no political parties, yet the line of demarcation was drawn before ever Washington was inaugurated. It is the little things which germinate . . . the birth of American party battles had risen in the problem of the titles by which the president, the cabinet and the Congress should be addressed. Next the social climbers, the snobbery, the appointment of Hamilton and Jefferson to the cabinet, the rise of Hamilton to a position of supremacy and with it the control of the infant government by the moneyed class. All still in the stage of experiment, and who, even today, can say that immediate success did not lie in the establishment of the Republic's finances and commercial credit? Alexander Hamilton we honor because of his master stroke for sound money, his genius for finance. Yet we must take into account the scandal of the day, the unconscionable profiteering of his followers— even some in Congress—in that same moneyed class who made veritable fortunes from the stupidity or the need or the lack of inside information on the part of the thousands of veterans, tradesmen, farmers or frontier settlers away from the larger seaport towns.

Slowly the lines were being formed. Within the cabinet itself Jefferson, a veritable Westerner of his day, mistrusting the fondness of Hamilton for his Chambers of Commerce and his contempt for the opinion of the masses; Hamilton, confident of his power, confident of the power of his leaders among merchants and aristocrats, wholly lacking in understanding or in fear of the rights of what he thought of as the rabble—the poor, the uneducated, the average human being who, even then, made up the mass of his countrymen.

The scene changes to Philadelphia, the next temporary capital. More display, greater snobbery, an increased assurance on the part of the men and women of wealth, of family, of commercial prestige; and, most important, a growth of the pro-British sentiment on the part of these, and an abhorrence for the successes and excesses of the onrushing French Revolution.

It is natural that in this environment the demarcation into parties grew apace. Jefferson, eclipsed in the cabinet by Hamilton, the natural democrat against the natural aristocrat, began then the mobilization of the masses against the autocracy of the few. It was a colossal task. With Hamilton were the organized compact forces of wealth, of birth, of commerce, of the press. With him at heart was Washington, the president. Jefferson could count only on the scattered raw material of the working masses, difficult to reach, more difficult to organize.

So began a warfare by press and pamphlet, skillfully forced by Jefferson and Madison and Freneau; bitterly answered by Hamilton and Ames and Fenno. A drawn battle of wits, perhaps, but every new reader a step toward the goal of Jefferson. A true public opinion was being made possible. . . .

So the ten years' drama drew to its curtain. Through all the mud-slinging, the abuse of power, the deliberate misrepresentation, Jefferson remained the calm philosopher. When troops were asked, it was Jefferson's followers who were the readiest to fall in on country's call. When grave questions of domestic policy arose, it was reserved for certain Federalists of New England to be the first to talk of the dissolution of the Union. Jefferson's faith in mankind was vindicated; his appeal to the intelligence of the average voter bore fruit; his conception of a democratic republic came true.

I have a breathless feeling as I lay down this book—a picture of escape after escape which this nation passed through in those first ten years; a picture of what might have been if the Republic had been finally organized as Alexander Hamilton sought. But I have a breathless feeling, too, as I wonder if, a century and a quarter later, the same contending forces are not again mobilizing. Hamiltons we have today. Is a Jefferson on the horizon?

3.

Whither Bound?

Speech to Milton Academy
Milton, Massachusetts, May 18, 1926

FDR would come to speak of democracy as "an everlasting march." In these remarks to the students at Milton Academy (published by Houghton Mifflin that same year), he made it very clear to the young men and women of the school that in contrast to many older folks he did not fear political and cultural change, but rather what might happen to the nation if the conservatives and reactionaries who governed the country in the 1920s remained in power and continued to stymie America's democratic progress.

In these two happy days with you at Milton, I have felt very deeply the close association of this gathering with the time, not long past, when all the schools of the nation gave the best of their manhood to a great cause. That crisis called for the highest ideals and received them. It is fitting that, when we who succeed meet in memory of those who died, high purpose to carry on their hopes should govern our thoughts.

After a war it is natural that a period of comparative rest should follow. But the World War brought forth so many new problems for all peoples that our peace must be a peace of action and constructive progress. The men who gave their lives would have had it so, and they call on us today to finish their task.

That is why I would speak chiefly of the future, for I am certain that those who served and died on the battlefields and on the seas gave great thought to the days to come.

So I ask the question: "Quo Vadis—Whither Bound?"

Forty or fifty years ago a certain citizen of this land was sorely troubled. Brought up in a Victorian atmosphere of gloomy religion, of copybook sentiment, of life by precept, he had lived essentially as had his fathers before him. Yet one day he fled to a far-off country. Sudden changes had come to affect his life and that of his neighbors; human voices were carried to him over a tiny copper wire, juggernauts called trolley cars lined his peaceful roads, steam was replacing sails, sputtering arc-lights were appearing in the comfortable darkness of his streets, machine-made goods were forcing out the loving craftsmanship of the centuries. But, more dangerous, the accepted social structure was becoming demoralized. Women—think of it, women!—were commencing to take positions in offices and industrial plants, and demanding—a very few of them—things called political rights; young people were actually questioning the age-long parental right to choose their mates for them; enjoyment and exercise on the Sabbath day were violating the code of generations of Christian ministers. Worst of all, a handful of these ministers themselves were openly rejecting formulas, and substituting a word called "love" for the old word called "charity." In politics, too, men were speaking of new ideals, and new parties, Populist and Socialist, were making themselves heard throughout the land.

"Surely," said he, "the nation cannot endure—I will flee from Sodom—the time is out of joint."

It matters not so much to my argument that this shirker fled as that his pending cataclysm has not yet fallen. Yet there are many like him who view the world today through his eyes—honest people, good people, educated people, influential people. Unrest in this world of ours is caused as much by those who fear change as by those who seek revolution; and unrest in any nation or in any organization, whether it be caused by ultra-conservatism or by extreme radicalism, is in the long run a healthy sign. In government, in science, in industry, in the arts, in action and apathy are the most potent foes.

It is necessary to look back before we look at today or the future: in this lies the truest value of the study of history. I well remember my old schoolmaster, Mr. Peabody, teaching us that material and spiritual progress has had its periodic ups and downs, but that the up-curves are always the longer, and that the net advance is certain in the end.

When the triumphs of Rome fell in a tide of barbarianism and the dark ages followed, civilization and Christianity were not blotted out. Working in unseen ways through many centuries they permeated into every corner of the Western world, and at last broke through the gloom into the glories of the Renaissance. They rose, not as a smoothly flowing tide, but as the result of a great conflict. Thousands died for their faith on both sides. A budding science was labeled witchcraft or heresy. The most modest beginnings of popular government were called unholy. The very study of economics or of philosophy was banned as dangerous to the existing order.

By the year 1500 civilization and progress and Christianity had again come into their own. There followed three hundred years which might be called a period of distribution and of assimilation of the Renaissance. It was the period of the peoples of the world getting to know each other: communication and trade between the different countries of Europe progressed enormously; America and Africa were colonized and the way made open to India and China.

Yet from 1500 to 1800 not many real changes were made in the lives of people. Speed of communication by land and sea showed little gain, and, except for a few great scientific discoveries like those of Newton, science as such was in the groping stage.

It was only in the realm of government, toward the close of the period, that startling events actually occurred. The American Revolution, followed by the French Revolution, marked a new epoch in their field, though their leaven has worked so slowly that the processes of acquiring representative government are still going on.

The next century, however, from 1800 to 1900, and especially its later quarter, gave to the civilized world more physical and mental shocks than any similar period of history. Science won the first practical victory with the advent of steam, first by revolutionizing land transportation, then ocean voyages, and finally industry itself. But the most important factor was the dissemination of education among a vastly larger percentage of the population than ever before. We are told that in the Europe of the fifteenth century, less than five percent of all people could fairly be graded above the rank of serfs, devoid of even what we would call the rudiments of any education at all. In the nineteenth century the average man and woman obtained at least some hope and possibility of acquiring knowledge.

Yet, when all is said and done, the great inventions of yesterday—steam, telegraph, telephone, electrical light and power, industrial machinery—had at first comparatively small effect upon the actual lives which people led. Homes in the country and in the city in, say, 1875, were not so very different from similar homes in 1775. . . .

It was during the last quarter of the last century that the tremendous strides of science first made themselves definitely felt in the average home; for it is in the home that the practical effect of change at last makes itself felt. Once started, this change seems to have gained momentum with each succeeding year, until we come to the point today when we can truly say that the lives of the great majority of people are more different from the lives of 1875 than were our grandfathers' lives from those of the year 1500.

To come down to the very recent past, there is justification for saying that there has occurred an even more rapid condition of change in the past ten years.

Viewed historically, then, why should anyone express surprise at the loud chorus of protest which rises today against what we call the ways of the modern generation? In the fifteenth century nations were rent asunder by actual wars over changes nothing like so great. Today we howl through the press, we seek legislative remedies, we organize new associations, but we do not go to war. That, at least, is one definite proof of progress.

My old neighbor on the Hudson River, Rip Van Winkle, went soundly asleep, and seemed annoyed, on waking up many years later, to find that the world was very different. Rip has many successors today—some old people, and, I am sorry to say, a good many middle-aged people and young people, too. They have not been physically asleep, but they have come to view the world with eyes of the past. They have pictured a world and a life which they have known and have liked; they have put a little halo around it and said, "This is mine by heritage and choice—I will protect it and oppose any change."

The next step for these modern Van Winkles is to justify conservatism by calling all who seek new things heretics or anarchists. Think how often the Bible has been called upon to justify repression of liberal thought; how often seekers after human rights have suffered persecution under the guise of man-made law. That is but natural—what is more wonderful is that Christianity is great enough and broad enough to throw off the control of dead hands and to march forward in step with the progress of mankind. So also with law—from time to time it seems a hopeless drag on progress; but in the end it proves sufficiently elastic to catch up.

That is why I sympathize little with those radicals who tell you that our religion is dead, that our government is basically wrong. The churches today are beginning to go along with the new scientific growth and are opening the way to a simpler faith, a deeper faith, a *happier* faith, than ever our forefathers held. In the methods of our governing, also, we have come to accept, or at least to discuss without fear, problems and methods formerly mentioned only by wild-eyed visionaries.

The difficulties which beset the steps of religion and government come from two sources: the solidarity of the opposition to a new outlook, and the lack of cohesion on the part of the liberal thinkers themselves.

Naturally every proposed change offers a number of methods of change, and over these methods the seekers of change disagree. On the other side there is but one method—straight opposition, and this welds together the satisfied and the fearful. Probably on any given problem of modern life, if a count or classification could be made, the out-and-out conservatives would be found to be in a distinct minority. Yet the majority would be so divided over the *means* by which to gain their ends that they could not present sufficient unity to obtain action. This has been the history of progress. Measured by years, the actual control of human affairs is in the hands of conservatives for longer periods than in those of liberals or radicals. When the latter do come into power, they translate the constantly working leaven of progress into law or custom or use, but rarely obtain enough time in control to make further economic or social experiments.

None of us, therefore, need feel surprise that the government of our own country, for instance, is conservative by far the greater part of the time. Our national danger is, however, not that it may for four years or eight years become liberal or even radical, but that it may suffer from too long a period of the do-nothing or reactionary standards. . . .

I have spoken of the up-and-down curves of history—or rather of the periods of quiescence followed by rushing, active progress. We are in the midst of one of the latter now. Are we at the end of it?

I think not . . . On the contrary, I believe that more new and startling developments will take place in the immediate future than in the immediate past. With these will come other great changes in the lives and doings and thoughts of the average man and woman. Can we, by artificial means, call a halt? Obviously not.

What, for example, do leaders of scientific thought and research tell us? First of all, that investigation and experimentation will not, cannot, cease, but that they are adding, day by day, in startling measure, to the results already obtained. . . .

Every trend of modern science is toward the greater unification of mankind. Already we go to the other end of the world to stop at their point of origin human diseases which, left unchecked, might spread to us. Factories everywhere are seeking location at the source of their raw materials. Isthmian canals are constructed for world commerce. Sociological problems are examined in the light of the experience of other nations. Backward peoples are made wards of those more advanced. Power is exported. Capital is international. Foreign affairs are discussed by the average citizen. Wars and armaments are the concern of more than kings.

Isolation of individual nations will be as difficult in this future as would be the isolation of New England or the South today. The same laws of the history of progress apply. First, the self-sufficient small community, then the grouping of several communities, then the small state, then the nation, then alliances between nations, and now a permanent congress of nations.

No person who truly visualizes the future doubts that we are at the threshold of an era of cooperative endeavor between peoples and continents. Economic progress—social, financial, industrial, agricultural—is forcing the issue. Science in every branch is working on international lines. Laws and government in each national unit are influenced by experiments in other units . . .

In such vein we could go on, not foretelling the future, but listing the possible developments of that future—and when we use that word "future" we speak of things that very easily may come to pass within our own lives. When they come—if they come—are you and I ready to meet them?

Therein is the thought which this coming generation asks itself, and because we are interested in this future of ours we seem sometimes intolerant to the older generation. We see great events occurring before our eyes, we picture great changes to come. It is our right so to do.

I see many rays of pure light in that future . . . I see not merely materialism—new inventions, new conditions, new words—I see something spiritual coming to you who will take part. Service to mankind has been much taught of late, and this word "service" is, like the material things, still in its infancy of development. True service will not come until all the world recognizes all the rest of the world as one big family. To help a fellow being just because he is a fellow being is not enough. We treat that help too much as a duty, too little as an interest. How many of us lend helping hands to people we do not like, people who do not "belong to our crowd," people whom we subconsciously hope we may never see again?

This old world of ours is still suffering from an ancient disease known as "class consciousness."

Slowly but certainly we are coming to accept people for what they are, not for what they appear or claim to be, not for what their parents were. This does not mean that environment and good parents and education, and even heredity, do not count. We have proved by science that bad heredity is often a handicap, and that is why even our devotees of pure science will give hearty support to every effort to keep the home, the influence of parents and early training on the highest possible plane.

Do not ever forget that Christ's greatest teaching was, "Thou shalt love thy neighbor as thyself." Certainly we are far from that goal. Yet we approach it little by little. . . .

I must confess to pride in this coming generation of men and women. You are thinking more deeply than ever we did. You are working out your own salvation in terms that are less selfish than ever before in the world. You are more in love with life, more keenly interested in your fellow beings. You seek causes, fundamentals. You try all manner of experiments, often to the horror of us, your parents. You play with fire openly where we did so in secret, and fewer of you get burned. You learn for interest's sake, not by precept. You live by what you think is right, not by code. Mistakes you will make, every individual and every group, but your errors will be forgiven you if the spirit in which you make them is of high purpose.

In the days to come the heritage of the earth will be yours, and perhaps we ancients will look down on you from the height of the everlasting knowledge and say, "Well done, boy!"

Then, perhaps, even the sluggards, even the unready, will bear witness that the time is not out of joint. No longer will the cry of the older days go up, "Hail, Caesar, we about to die salute you." Rather can we of today and of tomorrow, reverent in our purpose, strong in our hope, say, "Hail, Lord, we greet Thee, we about to live."

4.

The "Self-Supporting" Man or Woman Has Become . . . Extinct

First Inaugural Address as Governor of New York
Albany, New York, January 1, 1929

Roosevelt was elected governor of New York in 1928, on the eve of the Great Depression, and he would be reelected in 1930. In his first inaugural address, he spoke of his determination to lead a liberal and progressive administration that—recognizing the growing "interdependence" of all people—would pursue the "public good" and harness democratic government to enhance the material lives of working people urban and rural.

It is a proud thing to be a citizen of the state of New York, not because of our great population and our natural resources, nor on account of our industries, our trade, or our agricultural development, but because the citizens of this state, more than any other state in the Union, have grown to realize the interdependence on each other which modern civilization has created. . . .

I object to having this spirit of personal civil responsibility to the state and to the individual, which has placed New York in the lead as a progressive commonwealth, described as "humanitarian." It is far more than that. It is the recognition that our civilization cannot endure unless we, as individuals, realize our personal responsibility to and dependency on the rest of the world. For it is literally true that the "self-supporting" man or woman has become as extinct as the man of the stone age. Without the help of thousands of others, any one of us would die, naked and starved. Consider the bread upon our table, the clothes upon our backs, the luxuries that make life pleasant; how many men worked in sunlit fields, in dark mines, in the fierce heat of molten metal, and among the looms and wheels of countless factories, in order to create them for our use and enjoyment.

I am proud that we of this state have grown to realize this dependence, and, what is more important, have also come to know that we, as individuals, in our turn must give our time and our intelligence to help those who have helped us. To secure more of life's pleasures for the farmer; to guard the toilers in the factories and to ensure them a fair wage and protection from the dangers of their trades; to compensate them by adequate insurance for injuries received while working for us; to open the doors of knowledge to their children more widely; to aid those who are crippled and ill; to pursue with strict justice all evil persons who prey upon their fellow men; and at the same time, by intelligent and helpful sympathy, to lead wrong doers into right paths—all of these great aims of life are more fully realized here than in any other state in the Union. We have but started on the road, and we have far to go; but during the last six years in particular, the people of this state have shown their impatience of those who seek to make such things a football of politics or, by blind unintelligent obstruction, attempt to bar the road to progress. . . .

Each one of us must realize the necessity of our personal interest, not only toward our fellow citizens, but in the government itself. You must watch, as a public duty, what is done and what is not done at Albany. You must understand the issues that arise in the Legislature, and the recommendations made by your governor, and judge for yourselves if they are right or wrong. If you find them right it is your duty as citizens on next election day to repudiate those who oppose, and to support by your vote those who strive for their accomplishment.

I want to call particularly on the public press of this state in whose high standards I have the greatest confidence, to devote more space to the explanation and consideration of such legislation as may come up this year, for no matter how willing the individual citizen may be to support wise and progressive measures, it is only through the press, and I mean not only our great dailies but their smaller sisters in the rural districts, that our electorate can learn and understand what is going on.

There are many puzzling problems to be solved. I will here mention but three. In the brief time that I have been speaking to you, there has run to waste on their paths toward the sea, enough power from our rivers to have turned the wheels of a thousand factories, to have lit a million farmers' homes—power which nature has supplied us through the gift of God . . .

I should like to state clearly the outstanding features of the problem itself. First, it is agreed, I think, that the water power of the state should belong to all the people. There was, perhaps, some excuse for careless legislative gift of power sites in the days when it was of no seemingly great importance. There can be no such excuse now. The title to this power must vest forever in the people of this state. . . .

It is also the duty of our legislative bodies to see that this power, which belongs to all the people, is transformed into usable electrical energy and distributed to them at the lowest possible cost. It is our power; and no inordinate profits must be allowed to those who act as the people's agents in bringing this power to their homes and workshops. If we keep these two fundamental facts before us, half of the problem disappears.

There remains the technical question as to which of several methods will bring this power to our doors with the least expense.

Let me here make clear the three divisions of this technical side of the question.

First, the construction of the dams, the erection of power houses, and the installation of the turbines necessary to convert the force of the falling water into electricity.

Second, the construction of many thousands of miles of transmission lines to bring the current so produced to the smaller distributing centers throughout the state; and

Third, the final distribution of this power into thousands of homes and factories.

How much of this shall be undertaken by the state, how much of this carried out by properly regulated private enterprises, how much of this by some combination of the two, is the practical question that we have before us. And in the consideration of the question I want to warn the people of this state against too hasty assumption that mere regulation by public service commissions is, in itself, a sure guarantee of protection of the interests of the consumer. . . .

I, as your governor, will insist, and I trust with the support of the whole people, that there be no alienation of our possession of and title to our power sites, and that whatever method of distribution be adopted, there can be no possible legal thwarting of the protection of the people themselves from excessive profits on the part of anybody.

On another matter I tread perhaps a new path. The phrase, "rich man's justice," has become too common nowadays. So complicated has our whole legal machinery become through our attempt to mend antiquated substructures by constant patching of the legal procedure and the courts that justice is our most expensive commodity. That rich criminals too often escape punishment *is* a general belief of our people. The difficulty with which our citizens maintain their civil rights before the courts has not been made a matter of such public notice but is equally serious. It is my hope that within the next two years we will have begun to simplify and to cheapen justice for the people.

Lastly, I want to refer to the difficult situation to which in recent years a large part of the rural population of our state has come. With few exceptions it has not shared in the prosperity of the urban centers.

It is not enough to dismiss this problem with the generality that it is the result of changing economic conditions. It is time to take practical steps to relieve our farm population of unequal tax burdens; to install economies in the methods or local government; to devise sounder marketing; to stabilize what has been too much a speculative industry; and, finally, to encourage the use of each acre of our state for the purpose to which it is by nature most suited. I am certain that the cities will cooperate to this end, and that, more and more, we as citizens shall become state-minded.

May I, as your newly elected governor, appeal for your help, for your advice, and, when you feel it is needed, for your criticism? No man may be a successful governor without the full assistance of the people of his own commonwealth. . . .

There is a period in our history known in all our school books as the "Era of Good Feeling." It is my hope that we stand on the threshold of another such era in this state. For my part, I pledge that the business of the state will not be allowed to become involved in partisan politics and that I will not attempt to claim unfair advantage for my party or for myself, for the accomplishing of those things on which we are all agreed.

You have honored me greatly by selecting me as your Chief Executive. It is my hope that I will not fail you in this critical period of our history. I wish that you may have a continuance of good government and the happiest of New Years.

5.

The Forgotten Man

A Radio Address from Albany, New York
April 7, 1932

Roosevelt ran for the Democratic presidential nomination in 1932 to challenge incumbent Republican president Herbert Hoover. The Great Depression, which had hit the nation and the world in 1929, was continuing to wreck the American economy and devastate the lives of millions.

Like most Republicans, Hoover resisted the idea of using the powers of government to intervene in and regulate the economy. But FDR thought otherwise. As New York's governor, he had actively confronted the economic and social crisis through initiatives such as launching public-works projects to provide electricity to more homes and farms and recruiting unemployed men to work on environmental conservation. Based on his gubernatorial record, he spoke of both using government and mobilizing Americans not simply to stem the crisis, but also to spur recovery. In the course of the campaign, he called for legislation and programs to regulate financial transactions, create federal public-works projects, rehabilitate the nation's land and forests, and establish "old-age" insurance. And in this early campaign speech, he promised a presidency that would "build from the bottom up, not the top down," pursue policies to restore working and farming people's "purchasing power," and afford Americans the security of home and livelihood that he knew they yearned for.

Although I understand that I am talking under the auspices of the Democratic National Committee, I do not want to limit myself to politics. I do not want to feel that I am addressing an audience of Democrats or that I speak merely as a Democrat myself. The present condition of our national affairs is too serious to be viewed through partisan eyes for partisan purposes.

Fifteen years ago my public duty called me to an active part in a great national emergency, the World War. Success then was due to a leadership whose vision carried beyond the timorous and futile gesture of sending a tiny army of 150,000 trained soldiers and the regular navy to the aid of our allies. The generalship of that moment conceived of a whole nation mobilized for war, economic, industrial, social and military resources gathered into a vast unit capable of and actually in the process of throwing into the scales ten million men equipped with physical needs and sustained by the realization that behind them were the united efforts of 110,000,000 human beings. It was a great plan because it was built from bottom to top and not from top to bottom.

In my calm judgment, the nation faces today a more grave emergency than in 1917.

It is said that Napoleon lost the battle of Waterloo because he forgot his infantry—he staked too much upon the more spectacular but less substantial cavalry. The present administration in Washington provides a close parallel. It has either forgotten or it does not want to remember the infantry of our economic army.

These unhappy times call for the building of plans that rest upon the forgotten, the unorganized but the indispensable units of economic power for plans like those of 1917 that build from the bottom up and not from the top down, that put their faith once more in the forgotten man at the bottom of the economic pyramid.

Obviously, these few minutes tonight permit no opportunity to lay down the ten or a dozen closely related objectives of a plan to meet our present emergency, but I can draw a few essentials, a beginning in fact, of a planned program.

It is the habit of the unthinking to turn in times like this to the illusions of economic magic. People suggest that a huge expenditure of public funds by the federal government and by state and local governments will completely solve the unemployment problem. But it is clear that even if we could raise many billions of dollars and find definitely useful public works to spend these billions on, even all that money would not give employment to the seven million or ten million people who are out of work. Let us admit frankly that it would be only a stopgap. A real economic cure must go to the killing of the bacteria in the system rather than to the treatment of external symptoms.

How much do the shallow thinkers realize, for example, that approximately one-half of our whole population, fifty or sixty million people, earn their living by farming or in small towns whose existence immediately depends on farms? They have today lost their purchasing power. Why? They are receiving for farm products less than the cost to them of growing these farm products. The result of this loss of purchasing power is that many other millions of people engaged in industry in the cities cannot sell industrial products to the farming half of the nation. This brings home to every city worker that his own employment is directly tied up with the farmer's dollar. No nation can long endure half bankrupt. Main Street, Broadway, the mills, the mines will close if half the buyers are broke. I cannot escape the conclusion that one of the essential parts of a national program of restoration must be to restore purchasing power to the farming half of the country. Without this the wheels of railroads and of factories will not turn.

Closely associated with this first objective is the problem of keeping the home-owner and the farm-owner where he is, without being dispossessed through the foreclosure of his mortgage. His relationship to the great banks of Chicago and New York is pretty remote. The two-billion-dollar fund which President Hoover and the Congress have put at the disposal of the big banks, the railroads, and the corporations of the nation is not for him.

His is a relationship to his little local bank or local loan company. It is a sad fact that even though the local lender in many cases does not want to evict the farmer or home-owner by foreclosure proceedings, he is forced to do so in order to keep his bank or company solvent. Here should be an objective of government itself, to provide at least as much assistance to the little fellow as it is now giving to the large banks and corporations. That is another example of building from the bottom up.

One other objective closely related to the problem of selling American products is to provide a tariff policy based upon economic common sense rather than upon politics, hot air, and pull. This country during the past few years, culminating with the Hawley-Smoot Tariff in 1929, has compelled the world to build tariff fences so high that world trade is decreasing to the vanishing point. The value of goods internationally exchanged is today less than half of what it was three or four years ago.

Every man and woman who gives any thought to the subject knows that if our factories run even 80 percent of capacity, they will turn out more products than we as a nation can possibly use ourselves. The answer is that if they run on 80 percent of capacity, we must sell some goods abroad. How can we do that if the outside nations cannot pay us in cash? And we know by sad experience that they cannot do that. The only way they can pay us is in their own goods or raw materials, but this foolish tariff of ours makes that impossible.

What we must do is this: revise our tariff on the basis of a reciprocal exchange of goods, allowing other nations to buy and to pay for our goods by sending us such of their goods as will not seriously throw any of our industries out of balance, and incidentally making impossible in this country the continuance of pure monopolies which cause us to pay excessive prices for many of the necessities of life.

Such objectives as these three, restoring farmers' buying power, relief to the small banks and home-owners, and a reconstructed tariff policy, are only a part of ten or a dozen vital factors. But they seem to be beyond the concern of a national administration which can think in terms only of the top of the social and economic structure. It has sought temporary relief from the top down rather than permanent relief from the bottom up. . . .

It is high time to get back to fundamentals. It is high time to admit with courage that we are in the midst of an emergency at least equal to that of war. Let us mobilize to meet it.

6.

Bold, Persistent Experimentation

Campaign Speech at Oglethorpe University
Atlanta, Georgia, May 22, 1932

Campaigning for the presidency, Roosevelt not only lambasted the Hoover administration for its inaction and lack of a plan to lift the country out of depression, he also began to pose serious questions about the wastefulness of unregulated American capitalism. In this speech at Oglethorpe University, he promised to develop a plan that, instead of simply restoring the status quo of 1929, would apply the powers of democratic government to reform the national economy and raise consumers' purchasing power by redistributing America's national income.

President Jacobs, members and friends of Oglethorpe University, and especially you, my fellow members of the Class of 1932:

For me, as for you, this is a day of honorable attainment. . . . For many of you, doubtless, this mark of distinction which you have received today has meant greater sacrifice, by your parents or by yourselves, than you anticipated when you matriculated almost four years ago. The year 1928 does not seem far in the past, but since that time, as all of us are aware, the world about us has experienced significant changes. Four years ago, if you heard and believed the tidings of the time, you could expect to take your place in a society well supplied with material things and could look forward to the not too distant time when you would be living in your own homes, each (if you believed the politicians) with a two-car garage; and, without great effort, would be providing yourselves and your families with all the necessities and amenities of life, and perhaps in addition assure by your savings their security and your own in the future. Indeed, if you were observant, you would have seen that many of your elders had discovered a still easier road to material success. They had found that once they had accumulated a few dollars they needed only to put them in the proper place and then sit back and read in comfort the hieroglyphics called stock quotations which proclaimed that their wealth was mounting miraculously without any work or effort on their part. Many who were called and who are still pleased to call themselves the leaders of finance celebrated and assured us of an eternal future for this easy-chair mode of living. And to the stimulation of belief in this dazzling chimera were lent not only the voices of some of our public men in high office, but their influence and the material aid of the very instruments of government which they controlled.

How sadly different is the picture which we see around us today! If only the mirage had vanished, we should not complain, for we should all be better off. But with it have vanished, not only the easy gains of speculation, but much of the savings of thrifty and prudent men and women, put by for their old age and for the education of their children. With these savings has gone, among millions of our fellow citizens, that sense of security to which they have rightly felt they are entitled in a land abundantly endowed with natural resources and with productive facilities to convert them into the necessities of life for all of our population. More calamitous still, there has vanished with the expectation of future security the certainty of today's bread and clothing and shelter.

Some of you—I hope not many—are wondering today how and where you will be able to earn your living a few weeks or a few months hence. Much has been written about the hope of youth. I prefer to emphasize another quality. I hope that you who have spent four years in an institution whose fundamental purpose, I take it, is to train us to pursue truths relentlessly and to look at them courageously will face the unfortunate state of the world about you with greater clarity of vision than many of your elders.

As you have viewed this world of which you are about to become a more active part, I have no doubt that you have been impressed by its chaos, its lack of plan. Perhaps some of you have used stronger language. And stronger language is justified. Even had you been graduating, instead of matriculating, in these rose-colored days of 1928, you would, I believe, have perceived this condition. For beneath all the happy optimism of those days there existed lack of plan and a great waste.

This failure to measure true values and to look ahead extended to almost every industry, every profession, every walk of life. . . .

In the same way we cannot review carefully the history of our industrial advance without being struck with its haphazardness, the gigantic waste with which it has been accomplished, the superfluous duplication of productive facilities, the continual scrapping of still useful equipment, the tremendous mortality in industrial and commercial undertakings, the thousands of dead-end trails into which enterprise has been lured, the profligate waste of natural resources. Much of this waste is the inevitable by-product of progress in a society which values individual endeavor and which is susceptible to the changing tastes and customs of the people of which it is composed. But much of it, I believe, could have been prevented by greater foresight and by a larger measure of social planning. Such controlling and directive forces as have been developed in recent years reside to a dangerous degree in groups having special interests in our economic order, interests which do not coincide with the interests of the nation as a whole. I believe that the recent course of our history has demonstrated that, while we may utilize their expert knowledge of certain problems and the special facilities with which they are familiar, we cannot allow our economic life to be controlled by that small group of men whose chief outlook upon the social welfare is tinctured by the fact that they can make huge profits from the lending of money and the marketing of securities—an outlook which deserves the adjectives "selfish" and "opportunist."

You have been struck, I know, by the tragic irony of our economic situation today. We have not been brought to our present state by any natural calamity—by drought or floods or earthquakes or by the destruction of our productive machine or our manpower. Indeed, we have a superabundance of raw materials, a more than ample supply of equipment for manufacturing these materials into the goods which we need, and transportation and commercial facilities for making them available to all who need them. But raw materials stand unused, factories stand idle, railroad traffic continues to dwindle, merchants sell less and less, while millions of able-bodied men and women, in dire need, are clamoring for the opportunity to work. This is the awful paradox with which we are confronted, a stinging rebuke that challenges our power to operate the economic machine which we have created.

We are presented with a multitude of views as to how we may again set into motion that economic machine. Some hold to the theory that the periodic slowing down of our economic machine is one of its inherent peculiarities—a peculiarity which we must grin, if we can, and bear because if we attempt to tamper with it we shall cause even worse ailments. According to this theory, as I see it, if we grin and bear long enough, the economic machine will eventually begin to pick up speed and in the course of an indefinite number of years will again attain that maximum number of revolutions which signifies what we have been wont to miscall prosperity, but which, alas, is but a last ostentatious twirl of the economic machine before it again succumbs to that mysterious impulse to slow down again. This attitude toward our economic machine requires not only greater stoicism, but greater faith in immutable economic law and less faith in the ability of man to control what he has created than I, for one, have. Whatever elements of truth lie in it, it is an invitation to sit back and do nothing; and all of us are suffering today, I believe, because this comfortable theory was too thoroughly implanted in the minds of some of our leaders, both in finance and in public affairs.

Other students of economics trace our present difficulties to the ravages of the World War and its bequest of unsolved political and economic and financial problems. Still others trace our difficulties to defects in the world's monetary systems. Whether it be an original cause, an accentuating cause, or an effect, the drastic change in the value of our monetary unit in terms of the commodities is a problem which we must meet straightforwardly. It is self-evident that we must either restore commodities to a level approximating their dollar value of several years ago or else that we must continue the destructive process of reducing, through defaults or through deliberate writing down, obligations assumed at a higher price level.

Possibly because of the urgency and complexity of this phase of our problem, some of our economic thinkers have been occupied with it to the exclusion of other phases of as great importance.

Of these other phases, that which seems most important to me in the long run is the problem of controlling by adequate planning the creation and distribution of those products which our vast economic machine is capable of yielding. It is true that capital, whether public or private, is needed in the creation of new enterprise and that such capital gives employment.

But think carefully of the vast sums of capital or credit which in the past decade have been devoted to unjustified enterprises—to the development of unessentials and to the multiplying of many products far beyond the capacity of the nation to absorb. It is the same story as the thoughtless turning out of too many school teachers and too many lawyers.

Here again, in the field of industry and business many of those whose primary solicitude is confined to the welfare of what they call capital have failed to read the lessons of the past few years and have been moved less by calm analysis of the needs of the nation as a whole than by a blind determination to preserve their own special stakes in the economic order. I do not mean to intimate that we have come to the end of this period of expansion. We shall continue to need capital for the production of newly invented devices, for the replacement of equipment worn out or rendered obsolete by our technical progress; we need better housing in many of our cities and we still need in many parts of the country more good roads, canals, parks, and other improvements.

But it seems to me probable that our physical economic plant will not expand in the future at the same rate at which it has expanded in the past. We may build more factories, but the fact remains that we have enough now to supply all of our domestic needs, and more, if they are used. With these factories we can now make more shoes, more textiles, more steel, more radios, more automobiles, more of almost everything than we can use.

No, our basic trouble was not an insufficiency of capital. It was an insufficient distribution of buying power coupled with an oversufficient speculation in production. While wages rose in many of our industries, they did not as a whole rise proportionately to the reward to capital, and at the same time the purchasing power of other great groups of our population was permitted to shrink. We accumulated such a superabundance of capital that our great bankers were vying with each other, some of them employing questionable methods, in their efforts to lend this capital at home and abroad.

I believe that we are at the threshold of a fundamental change in our popular economic thought, that in the future we are going to think less about the producer and more about the consumer. Do what we may have to do to inject life into our ailing economic order, we cannot make it endure for long unless we can bring about a wiser, more equitable distribution of the national income.

It is well within the inventive capacity of man, who has built up this great social and economic machine capable of satisfying the wants of all, to ensure that all who are willing and able to work receive from it at least the necessities of life. In such a system, the reward for a day's work will have to be greater, on the average, than it has been, and the reward to capital, especially capital which is speculative, will have to be less. But I believe that after the experience of the last three years, the average citizen would rather receive a smaller return upon his savings in return for greater security for the principal, than experience for a moment the thrill or the prospect of being a millionaire only to find the next moment that his fortune, actual or expected, has withered in his hand because the economic machine has again broken down.

It is toward that objective that we must move if we are to profit by our recent experiences. Probably few will disagree that the goal is desirable. Yet many, of faint heart, fearful of change, sitting tightly on the rooftops in the flood, will sternly resist striking out for it, lest they fail to attain it. Even among those who are ready to attempt the journey there will be violent differences of opinion as to how it should be made. So complex, so widely distributed over our whole society are the problems which confront us that men and women of common aim do not agree upon the method of attacking them. Such disagreement leads to doing nothing, to drifting. Agreement may come too late.

Let us not confuse objectives with methods. Too many so-called leaders of the nation fail to see the forest because of the trees. Too many of them fail to recognize the vital necessity of planning for definite objectives. True leadership calls for the setting forth of the objectives and the rallying of public opinion in support of these objectives.

Do not confuse objectives with methods. When the nation becomes substantially united in favor of planning the broad objectives of civilization, then true leadership must unite thought behind definite methods.

The country needs and, unless I mistake its temper, the country demands bold, persistent experimentation. It is common sense to take a method and try it: If it fails, admit it frankly and try another. But above all, try something. The millions who are in want will not stand by silently forever while the things to satisfy their needs are within easy reach.

We need enthusiasm, imagination, and the ability to face facts, even unpleasant ones, bravely. We need to correct, by drastic means if necessary, the faults in our economic system from which we now suffer. We need the courage of the young. Yours is not the task of making your way in the world, but the task of remaking the world which you will find before you. May every one of us be granted the courage, the faith and the vision to give the best that is in us to that remaking!

7.

A New Deal for the American People

Speech to the Democratic National Convention
Chicago, Illinois, July 2, 1932

Upon winning the nomination, Roosevelt broke with tradition by flying from New York to Chicago to attend the Democratic National Convention and deliver his acceptance speech in person. In a rousing address that garnered enthusiastic applause, he declared that he fully appreciated that Americans most of all wanted "work and security"; announced he would seek the repeal of the Eighteenth Amendment (Prohibition); and, in essentially radical terms, debunked the long-prevailing idea that government should not intervene in the economy: "We must lay hold of the fact that economic laws are not made by nature. They are made by human beings."

Chairman Walsh, my friends of the Democratic National Convention of 1932:

I appreciate your willingness after these six arduous days to remain here, for I know well the sleepless hours which you and I have had. I regret that I am late, but I have no control over the winds of heaven and could only be thankful for my Navy training.

The appearance before a national convention of its nominee for president, to be formally notified of his selection, is unprecedented and unusual, but these are unprecedented and unusual times. I have started out on the tasks that lie ahead by breaking the absurd traditions that the candidate should remain in professed ignorance of what has happened for weeks until he is formally notified of that event many weeks later.

My friends, may this be the symbol of my intention to be honest and to avoid all hypocrisy or sham, to avoid all silly shutting of the eyes to the truth in this campaign. You have nominated me and I know it, and I am here to thank you for the honor.

Let it also be symbolic that in so doing I broke traditions. Let it be from now on the task of our Party to break foolish traditions. We will break foolish traditions and leave it to the Republican leadership, far more skilled in that art, to break promises.

Let us now and here highly resolve to resume the country's interrupted march along the path of real progress, of real justice, of real equality for all of our citizens, great and small . . .

I have many things on which I want to make my position clear at the earliest possible moment in this campaign. . . .

As we enter this new battle, let us keep always present with us some of the ideals of the Party: The fact that the Democratic Party by tradition and by the continuing logic of history, past and present, is the bearer of liberalism and of progress and at the same time of safety to our institutions. And if this appeal fails, remember well, my friends, that a resentment against . . . the failure of Republican leaders to solve our troubles may degenerate into unreasoning radicalism.

The great social phenomenon of this depression, unlike others before it, is that it has produced but a few of the disorderly manifestations that too often attend upon such times.

Wild radicalism has made few converts, and the greatest tribute that I can pay to my countrymen is that in these days of crushing want there persists an orderly and hopeful spirit on the part of the millions of our people who have suffered so much. To fail to offer them a new chance is not only to betray their hopes but to misunderstand their patience.

To meet by reaction that danger of radicalism is to invite disaster. Reaction is no barrier to the radical. It is a challenge, a provocation. The way to meet that danger is to offer a workable program of reconstruction, and the party to offer it is the party with clean hands.

This, and this only, is a proper protection against blind reaction on the one hand and an improvised, hit-or-miss, irresponsible opportunism on the other.

There are two ways of viewing the government's duty in matters affecting economic and social life. The first sees to it that a favored few are helped and hopes that some of their prosperity will leak through, sift through, to labor, to the farmer, to the small business man. That theory belongs to the party of Toryism, and I had hoped that most of the Tories left this country in 1776.

But it is not and never will be the theory of the Democratic Party. This is no time for fear, for reaction or for timidity. Here and now I invite those nominal Republicans who find that their conscience cannot be squared with the groping and the failure of their party leaders to join hands with us; here and now, in equal measure, I warn those nominal Democrats who squint at the future with their faces turned toward the past, and who feel no responsibility to the demands of the new time, that they are out of step with their Party.

Yes, the people of this country want a genuine choice this year, not a choice between two names for the same reactionary doctrine. Ours must be a party of liberal thought, of planned action, of enlightened international outlook, and of the greatest good to the greatest number of our citizens. . . .

I cannot take up all the problems today. I want to touch on a few that are vital. Let us look a little at the recent history and the simple economics, the kind of economics that you and I and the average man and woman talk.

In the years before 1929 we know that this country had completed a vast cycle of building and inflation; for ten years we expanded on the theory of repairing the wastes of the War, but actually expanding far beyond that, and also beyond our natural and normal growth. Now it is worth remembering, and the cold figures of finance prove it, that during that time there was little or no drop in the prices that the consumer had to pay, although those same figures proved that the cost of production fell very greatly; corporate profit resulting from this period was enormous; at the same time little of that profit was devoted to the reduction of prices. The consumer was forgotten. Very little of it went into increased wages; the worker was forgotten, and by no means an adequate proportion was even paid out in dividends—the stockholder was forgotten. . . .

What was the result? Enormous corporate surpluses piled up—the most stupendous in history. Where, under the spell of delirious speculation, did those surpluses go? Let us talk economics that the figures prove and that we can understand. Why, they went chiefly in two directions: first, into new and unnecessary plants which now stand stark and idle; and second, into the call-money market of Wall Street, either directly by the corporations, or indirectly through the banks. Those are the facts. Why blink at them?

Then came the crash. You know the story. Surpluses invested in unnecessary plants became idle. Men lost their jobs; purchasing power dried up; banks became frightened and started calling loans. Those who had money were afraid to part with it. Credit contracted. Industry stopped. Commerce declined, and unemployment mounted.

And there we are today.

Translate that into human terms. See how the events of the past three years have come home to specific groups of people: first, the group dependent on industry; second, the group dependent on agriculture; third, and made up in large part of members of the first two groups, the people who are called "small investors and depositors." In fact, the strongest possible tie between the first two groups, agriculture and industry, is the fact that the savings and to a degree the security of both are tied together in that third group—the credit structure of the nation.

Never in history have the interests of all the people been so united in a single economic problem. . . .

I propose to you, my friends, and through you, that government of all kinds, big and little, be made solvent and that the example be set by the president of the United States and his cabinet.

And talking about setting a definite example, I congratulate this convention for having had the courage fearlessly to write into its declaration of principles what an overwhelming majority here assembled really thinks about the Eighteenth Amendment. This convention wants repeal. Your candidate wants repeal. And I am confident that the United States of America wants repeal. . . .

I say to you now that from this date on the Eighteenth Amendment is doomed . . .

My friends, you and I as commonsense citizens know that it would help to protect the savings of the country from the dishonesty of crooks and from the lack of honor of some men in high financial places. Publicity is the enemy of crookedness.

And now one word about unemployment, and incidentally about agriculture. I have favored the use of certain types of public works as a further emergency means of stimulating employment and the issuance of bonds to pay for such public works, but I have pointed out that no economic end is served if we merely build without building for a necessary purpose. Such works, of course, should insofar as possible be self-sustaining if they are to be financed by the issuing of bonds. So as to spread the points of all kinds as widely as possible, we must take definite steps to shorten the working day and the working week.

Let us use common sense and business sense. Just as one example, we know that a very hopeful and immediate means of relief, both for the unemployed and for agriculture, will come from a wide plan of the converting of many millions of acres of marginal and unused land into timberland through reforestation. There are tens of millions of acres east of the Mississippi River alone in abandoned farms, in cut-over land, now growing up in worthless brush. Why, every European nation has a definite land policy, and has had one for generations. We have none. Having none, we face a future of soil erosion and timber famine. It is clear that economic foresight and immediate employment march hand in hand in the call for the reforestation of these vast areas.

In so doing, employment can be given to a million men. That is the kind of public work that is self-sustaining, and therefore capable of being financed by the issuance of bonds which are made secure by the fact that the growth of tremendous crops will provide adequate security for the investment.

Yes, I have a very definite program for providing employment by that means. I have done it, and I am doing it today in the state of New York. I know that the Democratic Party can do it successfully in the nation. That will put men to work, and that is an example of the action that we are going to have.

Now as a further aid to agriculture, we know perfectly well—but have we come out and said so clearly and distinctly?—we should repeal immediately those provisions of law that compel the federal government to go into the market to purchase, to sell, to speculate in farm products in a futile attempt to reduce farm surpluses. And they are the people who are talking of keeping government out of business. The practical way to help the farmer is by an arrangement that will, in addition to lightening some of the impoverishing burdens from his back, do something toward the reduction of the surpluses of staple commodities that hang on the market. It should be our aim to add to the world prices of staple products the amount of a reasonable tariff protection, to give agriculture the same protection that industry has today.

And in exchange for this immediately increased return I am sure that the farmers of this nation would agree ultimately to such planning of their production as would reduce the surpluses and make it unnecessary in later years to depend on dumping those surpluses abroad in order to support domestic prices. That result has been accomplished in other nations; why not in America, too? . . .

That is why we are going to make the voters understand this year that this nation is not merely a nation of independence, but it is, if we are to survive, bound to be a nation of interdependence—town and city, and north and south, east and west . . .

My program, of which I can only touch on these points, is based upon this simple moral principle: the welfare and the soundness of a nation depend first upon what the great mass of the people wish and need; and second, whether or not they are getting it.

What do the people of America want more than anything else? To my mind, they want two things: work, with all the moral and spiritual values that go with it; and with work, a reasonable measure of security—security for themselves and for their wives and children. Work and security—these are more than words. They are more than facts. They are the spiritual values, the true goal toward which our efforts of reconstruction should lead. These are the values that this program is intended to gain; these are the values we have failed to achieve by the leadership we now have.

Our Republican leaders tell us economic laws—sacred, inviolable, unchangeable—cause panics which no one could prevent. But while they prate of economic laws, men and women are starving. We must lay hold of the fact that economic laws are not made by nature. They are made by human beings.

Yes, when—not if—when we get the chance, the federal government will assume bold leadership in distress relief. . . .

I say that while primary responsibility for relief rests with localities now, as ever, yet the federal government has always had and still has a continuing responsibility for the broader public welfare. It will soon fulfill that responsibility. . . .

One word more: Out of every crisis, every tribulation, every disaster, mankind rises with some share of greater knowledge, of higher decency, of purer purpose. Today we shall have come through a period of loose thinking, descending morals, an era of selfishness, among individual men and women and among nations. Blame not governments alone for this. Blame ourselves in equal share. Let us be frank in acknowledgment of the truth that many amongst us have made obeisance to Mammon, that the profits of speculation, the easy road without toil, have lured us from the old barricades. To return to higher standards we must abandon the false prophets and seek new leaders of our own choosing.

Never before in modern history have the essential differences between the two major American parties stood out in such striking contrast as they do today. Republican leaders not only have failed in material things, they have failed in national vision, because in disaster they have held out no hope, they have pointed out no path for the people below to climb back to places of security and of safety in our American life.

Throughout the nation, men and women, forgotten in the political philosophy of the government of the last years, look to us here for guidance and for more equitable opportunity to share in the distribution of national wealth.

On the farms, in the large metropolitan areas, in the smaller cities and in the villages, millions of our citizens cherish the hope that their old standards of living and of thought have not gone forever. Those millions cannot and shall not hope in vain.

I pledge you, I pledge myself, to a new deal for the American people. Let us all here assembled constitute ourselves prophets of a new order of competence and of courage. This is more than a political campaign; it is a call to arms. Give me your help, not to win votes alone, but to win in this crusade to restore America to its own people.

8.

Every Man Has a Right to Life: An Economic Declaration of Rights

Speech to the Commonwealth Club
San Francisco, California, September 23, 1932

Though Roosevelt never wrote the history of the United States he had projected, he cultivated a democratic narrative of America through his speeches that regularly reached from the Revolution to his own day and into the future. In this address at the Commonwealth Club in San Francisco, he spoke proudly of the growth of the American economy and the development of the nation's industrial strength. But, noting how power and wealth had become concentrated in the hands of a few, and the promise of life, liberty, and the pursuit of happiness proclaimed in the Declaration of Independence was being denied to too many Americans, he called for the creation of a new Declaration, an "economic declaration of rights," to renew America's founding promise—which was an idea that would remain central to his thinking and powerfully inform his vision of the Four Freedoms (1941) and ensuing call for an Economic Bill of Rights (1944) for all Americans.

My friends:

I count it a privilege to be invited to address the Commonwealth Club. It has stood in the life of this city and state and, it is perhaps accurate to add, the nation, as a group of citizen leaders interested in fundamental problems of government, and chiefly concerned with achievement of progress in government through nonpartisan means. The privilege of addressing you, therefore, in the heat of a political campaign, is great. I want to respond to your courtesy in terms consistent with your policy.

I want to speak not of politics but of government. I want to speak not of parties, but of universal principles. They are not political, except in that larger sense in which a great American once expressed a definition of politics, that nothing in all of human life is foreign to the science of politics. . . .

Sometimes, my friends, particularly in years such as these, the hand of discouragement falls upon us. It seems that things are in a rut, fixed, settled, that the world has grown old and tired and very much out of joint. This is the mood of depression, of dire and weary depression.

But then we look around us in America, and everything tells us that we are wrong. America is new. It is in the process of change and development. It has the great potentialities of youth, and particularly is this true of the great West, and of this coast, and of California . . .

I want to invite you, therefore, to consider with me in the large, some of the relationships of government and economic life that go deeply into our daily lives, our happiness, our future and our security.

The issue of government has always been whether individual men and women will have to serve some system of government or economics, or whether a system of government and economics exists to serve individual men and women. This question has persistently dominated the discussion of government for many generations. On questions relating to these things men have differed, and for time immemorial it is probable that honest men will continue to differ.

The final word belongs to no man; yet we can still believe in change and in progress. Democracy, as a dear old friend of mine in Indiana, Meredith Nicholson, has called it, is a quest, a never-ending seeking for better things, and in the seeking for these things and the striving for them, there are many roads to follow. But, if we map the course of these roads, we find that there are only two general directions.

When we look about us, we are likely to forget how hard people have worked to win the privilege of government. . . .

But the creators of national government were perforce ruthless men. . . .

There came a growing feeling that government was conducted for the benefit of a few who thrived unduly at the expense of all. The people sought a balancing—a limiting force. There came gradually, through town councils, trade guilds, national parliaments, by constitution and by popular participation and control, limitations on arbitrary power.

Another factor that tended to limit the power of those who ruled was the rise of the ethical conception that a ruler bore a responsibility for the welfare of his subjects.

The American colonies were born in this struggle. The American Revolution was a turning point in it. After the Revolution the struggle continued and shaped itself in the public life of the country. There were those who because they had seen the confusion which attended the years of war for American independence surrendered to the belief that popular government was essentially dangerous and essentially unworkable. They were honest people, my friends, and we cannot deny that their experience had warranted some measure of fear. The most brilliant, honest and able exponent of this point of view was Hamilton. He was too impatient of slow-moving methods.

Fundamentally he believed that the safety of the republic lay in the autocratic strength of its government, that the destiny of individuals was to serve that government, and that fundamentally a great and strong group of central institutions, guided by a small group of able and public-spirited citizens, could best direct all government.

But Mr. Jefferson, in the summer of 1776, after drafting the Declaration of Independence turned his mind to the same problem and took a different view. He did not deceive himself with outward forms. Government to him was a means to an end, not an end in itself; it might be either a refuge and a help or a threat and a danger, depending on the circumstances. . . .

You are familiar with the great political duel which followed; and how Hamilton, and his friends, building toward a dominant centralized power, were at length defeated in the great election of 1800, by Mr. Jefferson's party. Out of that duel came the two parties, Republican and Democratic, as we know them today.

So began, in American political life, the new day, the day of the individual against the system, the day in which individualism was made the great watchword of American life. The happiest of economic conditions made that day long and splendid. On the Western frontier, land was substantially free. No one, who did not shirk the task of earning a living, was entirely without opportunity to do so. Depressions could, and did, come and go; but they could not alter the fundamental fact that most of the people lived partly by selling their labor and partly by extracting their livelihood from the soil, so that starvation and dislocation were practically impossible. At the very worst there was always the possibility of climbing into a covered wagon and moving west where the untilled prairies afforded a haven for men to whom the East did not provide a place. So great were our natural resources that we could offer this relief not only to our own people, but to the distressed of all the world; we could invite immigration from Europe, and welcome it with open arms. Traditionally, when a depression came a new section of land was opened in the West; and even our temporary misfortune served our manifest destiny.

It was in the middle of the nineteenth century that a new force was released and a new dream created. The force was what is called the industrial revolution, the advance of steam and machinery and the rise of the forerunners of the modern industrial plant. The dream was the dream of an economic machine, able to raise the standard of living for everyone; to bring luxury within the reach of the humblest; to annihilate distance by steam power and later by electricity, and to release everyone from the drudgery of the heaviest manual toil. It was to be expected that this would necessarily affect government. Heretofore, government had merely been called upon to produce conditions within which people could live happily, labor peacefully, and rest secure. Now it was called upon to aid in the consummation of this new dream. There was, however, a shadow over the dream. To be made real, it required use of the talents of men of tremendous will and tremendous ambition, since by no other force could the problems of financing and engineering and new developments be brought to a consummation.

So manifest were the advantages of the machine age, however, that the United States fearlessly, cheerfully, and, I think, rightly, accepted the bitter with the sweet. It was thought that no price was too high to pay for the advantages which we could draw from a finished industrial system. The history of the last half century is accordingly in large measure a history of a group of financial titans, whose methods were not scrutinized with too much care, and who were honored in proportion as they produced the results, irrespective of the means they used. The financiers who pushed the railroads to the Pacific were always ruthless, often wasteful, and frequently corrupt; but they did build railroads, and we have them today. It has been estimated that the American investor paid for the American railway system more than three times over in the process; but despite this fact the net advantage was to the United States. As long as we had free land; as long as population was growing by leaps and bounds; as long as our industrial plants were insufficient to supply our own needs, society chose to give the ambitious man free play and unlimited reward provided only that he produced the economic plant so much desired.

During this period of expansion, there was equal opportunity for all and the business of government was not to interfere but to assist in the development of industry. This was done at the request of business men themselves. The tariff was originally imposed for the purpose of "fostering our infant industry," a phrase I think the older among you will remember as a political issue not so long ago. The railroads were subsidized, sometimes by grants of money, oftener by grants of land; some of the most valuable oil lands in the United States were granted to assist the financing of the railroad which pushed through the Southwest. A nascent merchant marine was assisted by grants of money, or by mail subsidies, so that our steam shipping might ply the seven seas.

Some of my friends tell me that they do not want the government in business. With this I agree; but I wonder whether they realize the implications of the past. For while it has been American doctrine that the government must not go into business in competition with private enterprises, still it has been traditional, particularly in Republican administrations, for business urgently to ask the government to put at private disposal all kinds of government assistance. The same man who tells you that he does not want to see the government interfere in business—and he means it, and has plenty of good reasons for saying so—is the first to go to Washington and ask the government for a prohibitory tariff on his product. When things get just bad enough, as they did two years ago, he will go with equal speed to the United States government and ask for a loan; and the Reconstruction Finance Corporation is the outcome of it. Each group has sought protection from the government for its own special interests, without realizing that the function of government must be to favor no small group at the expense of its duty to protect the rights of personal freedom and of private property of all its citizens.

In retrospect we can now see that the turn of the tide came with the turn of the century. We were reaching our last frontier; there was no more free land and our industrial combinations had become great uncontrolled and irresponsible units of power within the state. Clear-sighted men saw with fear the danger that opportunity would no longer be equal; that the growing corporation, like the feudal baron of old, might threaten the economic freedom of individuals to earn a living. In that hour, our antitrust laws were born. The cry was raised against the great corporations. . . .

A glance at the situation today only too clearly indicates that equality of opportunity as we have known it no longer exists. Our industrial plant is built; the problem just now is whether under existing conditions it is not overbuilt. Our last frontier has long since been reached, and there is practically no more free land. More than half of our people do not live on the farms or on lands and cannot derive a living by cultivating their own property. There is no safety valve in the form of a Western prairie to which those thrown out of work by the Eastern economic machines can go for a new start. We are not able to invite the immigration from Europe to share our endless plenty. We are now providing a drab living for our own people.

Our system of constantly rising tariffs has at last reacted against us to the point of closing our Canadian frontier on the north, our European markets on the east, many of our Latin-American markets to the south, and a goodly proportion of our Pacific markets on the west, through the retaliatory tariffs of those countries. It has forced many of our great industrial institutions which exported their surplus production to such countries, to establish plants in such countries, within the tariff walls. This has resulted in the reduction of the operation of their American plants, and opportunity for employment.

Just as freedom to farm has ceased, so also the opportunity in business has narrowed. It still is true that men can start small enterprises, trusting to native shrewdness and ability to keep abreast of competitors; but area after area has been preempted altogether by the great corporations, and even in the fields which still have no great concerns, the small man starts under a handicap. The unfeeling statistics of the past three decades show that the independent business man is running a losing race.... Put plainly, we are steering a steady course toward economic oligarchy, if we are not there already.

Clearly, all this calls for a reappraisal of values. A mere builder of more industrial plants, a creator of more railroad systems, an organizer of more corporations, is as likely to be a danger as a help. The day of the great promoter or the financial titan, to whom we granted anything if only he would build, or develop, is over. Our task now is not discovery or exploitation of natural resources, or necessarily producing more goods. It is the soberer, less dramatic business of administering resources and plants already in hand, of seeking to reestablish foreign markets for our surplus production, of meeting the problem of underconsumption, of adjusting production to consumption, of distributing wealth and products more equitably, of adapting existing economic organizations to the service of the people. The day of enlightened administration has come.

Just as in older times the central government was first a haven of refuge, and then a threat, so now in a closer economic system the central and ambitious financial unit is no longer a servant of national desire, but a danger. I would draw the parallel one step farther. We did not think because national government had become a threat in the eighteenth century that therefore we should abandon the principle of national government. Nor today should we abandon the principle of strong economic units called corporations, merely because their power is susceptible of easy abuse. In other times we dealt with the problem of an unduly ambitious central government by modifying it gradually into a constitutional democratic government. So today we are modifying and controlling our economic units.

As I see it, the task of government in its relation to business is to assist the development of an economic declaration of rights, an economic constitutional order. This is the common task of statesman and business man. It is the minimum requirement of a more permanently safe order of things.

Happily, the times indicate that to create such an order not only is the proper policy of government, but it is the only line of safety for our economic structures as well. We know, now, that these economic units cannot exist unless prosperity is uniform, that is, unless purchasing power is well distributed throughout every group in the nation. That is why even the most selfish of corporations for its own interest would be glad to see wages restored and unemployment ended and to bring the Western farmer back to his accustomed level of prosperity and to assure a permanent safety to both groups. That is why some enlightened industries themselves endeavor to limit the freedom of action of each man and business group within the industry in the common interest of all; why business men everywhere are asking a form of organization which will bring the scheme of things into balance, even though it may in some measure qualify the freedom of action of individual units within the business.

The exposition need not further be elaborated. It is brief and incomplete, but you will be able to expand it in terms of your own business or occupation without difficulty. I think everyone who has actually entered the economic struggle—which means everyone who was not born to safe wealth—knows in his own experience and his own life that we have now to apply the earlier concepts of American government to the conditions of today.

The Declaration of Independence discusses the problem of government in terms of a contract. Government is a relation of give and take, a contract, perforce, if we would follow the thinking out of which it grew. Under such a contract rulers were accorded power, and the people consented to that power on consideration that they be accorded certain rights. The task of statesmanship has always been the redefinition of these rights in terms of a changing and growing social order. New conditions impose new requirements upon government and those who conduct government . . .

I feel that we are coming to a view through the drift of our legislation and our public thinking in the past quarter century that private economic power is, to enlarge an old phrase, a public trust as well. I hold that continued enjoyment of that power by any individual or group must depend upon the fulfillment of that trust. The men who have reached the summit of American business life know this best; happily, many of these urge the binding quality of this greater social contract.

The terms of that contract are as old as the Republic, and as new as the new economic order. Every man has a right to life; and this means that he has also a right to make a comfortable living. He may by sloth or crime decline to exercise that right; but it may not be denied him. We have no actual famine or dearth; our industrial and agricultural mechanism can produce enough and to spare. Our government formal and informal, political and economic, owes to everyone an avenue to possess himself of a portion of that plenty sufficient for his needs, through his own work.

Every man has a right to his own property; which means a right to be assured, to the fullest extent attainable, in the safety of his savings. By no other means can men carry the burdens of those parts of life which, in the nature of things, afford no chance of labor; childhood, sickness, old age. In all thought of property, this right is paramount; all other property rights must yield to it. If, in accord with this principle, we must restrict the operations of the speculator, the manipulator, even the financier, I believe we must accept the restriction as needful, not to hamper individualism but to protect it.

These two requirements must be satisfied, in the main, by the individuals who claim and hold control of the great industrial and financial combinations which dominate so large a part of our industrial life. They have undertaken to be, not business men, but princes of property. I am not prepared to say that the system which produces them is wrong. I am very clear that they must fearlessly and competently assume the responsibility which goes with the power. So many enlightened business men know this that the statement would be little more than a platitude, were it not for an added implication.

This implication is, briefly, that the responsible heads of finance and industry instead of acting each for himself, must work together to achieve the common end. They must, where necessary, sacrifice this or that private advantage; and in reciprocal self-denial must seek a general advantage. It is here that formal government—political government, if you choose—comes in. Whenever in the pursuit of this objective the lone wolf, the unethical competitor, the reckless promoter, the Ishmael or Insull whose hand is against every man's, declines to join in achieving an end recognized as being for the public welfare, and threatens to drag the industry back to a state of anarchy, the government may properly be asked to apply restraint. Likewise, should the group ever use its collective power contrary to the public welfare, the government must be swift to enter and protect the public interest.

The government should assume the function of economic regulation only as a last resort, to be tried only when private initiative, inspired by high responsibility, with such assistance and balance as government can give, has finally failed. As yet there has been no final failure, because there has been no attempt; and I decline to assume that this Nation is unable to meet the situation.

The final term of the high contract was for liberty and the pursuit of happiness. We have learned a great deal of both in the past century. We know that individual liberty and individual happiness mean nothing unless both are ordered in the sense that one man's meat is not another man's poison. We know that the old "rights of personal competency," the right to read, to think, to speak, to choose and live a mode of life, must be respected at all hazards. We know that liberty to do anything which deprives others of those elemental rights is outside the protection of any compact; and that government in this regard is the maintenance of a balance, within which every individual may have a place if he will take it; in which every individual may find safety if he wishes it; in which every individual may attain such power as his ability permits, consistent with his assuming the accompanying responsibility. . . .

Faith in America, faith in our tradition of personal responsibility, faith in our institutions, faith in ourselves demand that we recognize the new terms of the old social contract. We shall fulfill them, as we fulfilled the obligation of the apparent Utopia which Jefferson imagined for us in 1776, and which Jefferson, Roosevelt, and Wilson sought to bring to realization. We must do so, lest a rising tide of misery, engendered by our common failure, engulf us all. But failure is not an American habit; and in the strength of great hope we must all shoulder our common load.

9.

Social Justice Through Social Action

Campaign Address
Detroit, Michigan, October 2, 1932

Roosevelt was a man of great faith—faith in God, faith in America, and faith in his fellow citizens. And as he saw it, his Christian faith commanded him to pursue the cause of social justice. In this campaign speech, delivered on a Sunday in the form of a sermon, he decried the "trickle-down" theory of prosperity in which the rich get richer and the rest hope for the best and insisted—linking spiritual arms with liberal-minded Catholic, Protestant, and Jewish clergy—on the need for social action, indeed public action, to reduce poverty and improve the lives of all Americans.

My old friend Mayor Murphy, my old friend Governor Comstock, and you—many of you—my old friends of Detroit and of Michigan:

You know today is Sunday, and I am afraid that some of you people today in Detroit have been talking politics. Well, I am not going to. I want to talk to you about government. That is a very different thing. And I am not going to refer to parties at all.

I am going to refer to some of the fundamentals that antedate parties, and antedate republics and empires, fundamentals that are as old as mankind itself. They are fundamentals that have been expressed in philosophies, for I don't know how many thousands of years, in every part of the world. Today, in our boasted modern civilization, we are facing just exactly the same problem, just exactly the same conflict between two schools of philosophy that they faced in the earliest days of America, and indeed of the world. One of them—one of these old philosophies—is the philosophy of those who would "let things alone." The other is the philosophy that strives for something new—something that the human race has never attained yet, but something which I believe the human race can and will attain—social justice, through social action. . . .

In which school do you believe?

In the same way, there are two theories of prosperity and of well-being: The first theory is that if we make the rich richer, somehow they will let a part of their prosperity trickle down to the rest of us. The second theory—and I suppose this goes back to the days of Noah—I won't say Adam and Eve, because they had a less complicated situation—but, at least, back in the days of the flood, there was the theory that if we make the average of mankind comfortable and secure, their prosperity will rise upward, just as yeast rises up, through the ranks.

Now, my friends, the philosophy of social justice that I am going to talk about this Sabbath day, the philosophy of social justice through social action, calls definitely, plainly, for the reduction of poverty. And what do we mean when we talk about the reduction of poverty? We mean the reduction of the causes of poverty. When we have an epidemic of disease in these modern days, what do we do? We turn in the first instance to find out the sources from which the disease has come; and when we have found those sources, those causes, we turn the energy of our attack upon them.

We have got beyond the point in modern civilization of merely trying to fight an epidemic of disease by taking care of the victims after they are stricken. We do that; but we do more. We seek to prevent it; and the attack on poverty is not very unlike the attack on disease. We are seeking the causes and when we have found them, we must turn our attack upon them. What are the causes that destroy human beings, driving millions of them to destruction? Well, there are a good many of them, and there are a good many of us who are alive today who have seen tremendous steps taken toward the eradication of those causes.

Take, for instance, ill health: You and I know what has been accomplished by community effort, state effort, and the efforts and association of individual men and women toward the bettering of the health of humanity.

We have spent vast sums upon research. We have established a wholly new science, the science of public health; and we are carrying what we call today "instruction in health" into the most remote corners of our cities and our country districts. Apart from the humanitarian aspect, the result has been an economic saving. It has been money which has been returned to the community a thousand times over. You and I know that a sick person—a man, woman or child, who has to be taken care of—not only takes the individual who is sick out of active participation and useful citizenship, but takes somebody else, too. And so, from the purely dollars and cents point of view that we Americans are so fond of thinking about, public health has paid for itself.

And what have we done along other lines for the prevention of some of the causes of poverty?

I go back twenty-two years to a time when, in my state of New York, we tried to pass in the legislature what we called a Workmen's Compensation Act, knowing, as we did, that there were thousands of men and women who every year were seriously injured in industrial accidents of one kind or another, who became a burden on their community, who were unable to work, unable to get adequate medical care. A lot of us youngsters in the legislature in those days were called radicals. We were called Socialists. They did not know the word "Bolshevik" in those days, but if they had known that, we would have been called that, too. We put through a Workmen's Compensation Act. The courts, thinking in terms of the seventeenth century, as some courts do, declared it to be unconstitutional. So we had to go about amending the Constitution, and the following year we got a Workmen's Compensation Act . . .

Take another form of poverty in the old days. Not so long ago, there were in every part of the nation—in country districts and in city districts—hundreds and thousands of crippled children who could get no adequate care, who were lost to the community and who were a burden on the community. We have, in these past twenty or thirty years, gradually provided means for restoring crippled children to useful citizenship; and it has all been a factor in going after and solving one of the causes of poverty and disease.

And then in these later years, we have been wondering about old people; and we have come to the conclusion in this modern civilization that the old-fashioned theory of carting old people off to the county poorhouse is not the best thing after all. . . .

That sold me on the idea of trying to keep homes intact for old people. . . .

Now, those are some of the causes that have destroyed in past ages countless thousands of our fellow human beings. They are the causes that we must attack if we are to make the future safer for humanity. We can go on taking care of the handicapped and the crippled and the sick and the feeble-minded and the unemployed; but common sense and humanity call on us to turn our back definitely on these destroyers. Poverty resulting from these destroyers is largely preventable, but, my friends, if poverty is to be prevented, we require a broad program of social justice.

We cannot go back to the old prisons, for example, to the old systems of mere punishment under which a man out of prison was not fitted to live in our community alongside of us. We cannot go back to the old system of asylums. We cannot go back to the old lack of hospitals, the lack of public health. We cannot go back to the sweatshops of America. We cannot go back to children working in factories. Those days are gone.

There are a lot of new steps to take. It is not a question of just not going back. It is a question also of not standing still.

For instance, the problem of unemployment in the long run—and I am not talking about the emergency of this year—can be and shall be solved by the human race. Some leaders have wisely declared for a system of unemployment insurance throughout this broad land of ours; and we are going to come to it.

But I do not believe the Secretary of the Interior would be for it. He would say that great good is coming to this country because of the present situation. Yes, the followers of the philosophy of "let alone" have been decrying all of these measures of social welfare. What do they call them? They call them "paternalistic." All right, if they are paternalistic, I am a father.

They maintain that these laws interfere with individualism, forgetful of the fact that the causes of poverty in the main are beyond the control of any one individual or any czar, either a czar of politics or a czar of industry. The followers of the philosophy of "social action for the prevention of poverty" maintain that if we set up a system of justice we shall have small need for the exercise of mere philanthropy. Justice, after all, is the first goal we seek. We believe that when justice has been done individualism will have a greater security to devote the best that individualism itself can give. In other words, my friends, our long-range objective is not a dole, but a job.

At the same time, we have throughout this nation and I know you have in Detroit, because Frank Murphy has talked to me of it many times in the past year or two—widespread suffering which all of us in the city and country alike have to do everything we can to tide over. All agree that the first responsibility for the alleviation of poverty and distress and for the care of the victims of the depression rests upon the locality—its individuals, organizations and Government. It rests, first of all, perhaps, upon the private agencies of philanthropy, secondly, other social organizations, and last, but not least, the Church. Yet all agree that to leave to the locality the entire responsibility would result in placing the heaviest burden in most cases upon those who are the least able to bear it. In other words, the communities that have the most difficult problem, like Detroit, would be the communities that would have to bear the heaviest of the burdens.

And so the state should step in to equalize the burden by providing for a large portion of the care of the victims of poverty and by providing assistance and guidance for local communities.

Above and beyond that duty of the states the national government has a responsibility.

I would like to enlarge on that a lot, but that would be politics, and I cannot. My friends, the ideal of social justice of which I have spoken—an ideal that years ago might have been thought over-advanced—is now accepted by the moral leadership of all of the great religious groups of the country. Radical? Yes, and I shall show you how radical it is. I am going to cite three examples of what the churches say, the radical churches of America—Protestant, Catholic, and Jewish.

And first I will read to you from the Sunday sermon, the Labor Sermon sent out this year by the Federal Council of Churches of Christ in America, representing a very large proportion of the Protestants in our country.

Hear how radical they are: They say, "The thing that matters in any industrial system is what it does actually to human beings. . . .

"It is not denied that many persons of wealth are rendering great service to society. It is only suggested that the wealthy are overpaid in sharp contrast with the underpaid masses of the people. The concentration of wealth carries with it a dangerous concentration of power. It leads to conflict and violence. To suppress the symptoms of this inherent conflict while leaving the fundamental causes of it untouched is neither sound statesmanship nor Christian good-will.

"It is becoming more and more clear that the principles of our religion and the findings of social sciences point in the same direction. Economists now call attention to the fact that the present distribution of wealth and income, which is so unbrotherly in the light of Christian ethics, is also unscientific in that it does not furnish purchasing power to the masses to balance consumption and production in our machine age."

And now I am going to read you another great declaration and I wonder how many people will call it radical. It is just as radical as I am. It is a declaration from one of the greatest forces of conservatism in the world, the Catholic Church. I quote, my friends, from the scholarly encyclical issued last year by the Pope, one of the greatest documents of modern times:

"It is patent in our days that not alone is wealth accumulated, but immense power and despotic economic domination are concentrated in the hands of a few, and that those few are frequently not the owners but only the trustees and directors of invested funds which they administer at their good pleasure. . . .

"This accumulation of power, the characteristic note of the modern economic order, is a natural result of limitless free competition, which permits the survival of those only who are the strongest, which often means those who fight most relentlessly, who pay least heed to the dictates of conscience.

"This concentration of power has led to a three-fold struggle for domination: First, there is the struggle for dictatorship in the economic sphere itself; then the fierce battle to acquire control of the Government, so that its resources and authority may be abused in the economic struggle, and, finally, the clash between the Governments themselves."

And finally, I would read to you from another great statement, a statement from Rabbi Edward L. Israel, chairman of the Social Justice Commission of the Central Conference of American Rabbis. Here is what he says:

"We talk of the stabilization of business. What we need is the stabilization of human justice and happiness and the permanent employment of economic policies which will enable us to preserve the essential human values of life amid all the changing aspects of the economic order. We must have a revamping of the entire method of approach to these problems of the economic order. We need a new type of social conscience that will give us courage to act. . . .

"We so easily forget. Once the cry of so-called prosperity is heard in the land, we all become so stampeded by the spirit of the god Mammon, that we cannot serve the dictates of social conscience. . . . We are here to serve notice that the economic order is the invention of man; and that it cannot dominate certain eternal principles of justice and of God."

And so, my friends, I feel a little as if I had been preaching a sermon. I feel a little as if I had been talking too much of some of the fundamentals, and yet those fundamentals enter into your life and my life every day. More, perhaps, than we can realize. If we realized that far more, it would result throughout this country in a greater activity, a greater interest on the part of the individual men and women who make up our nation, in some of the problems which cannot be solved in the long run without the help of everybody.

We need leadership, of course. We need leadership of people who are honest in their thinking and honest in their doing. We need leadership, if it is straight thinking and unselfish; but in the last analysis we must have the help of the men and women all the way from the top to the bottom, especially of the men and women who believe in the school of philosophy which is not content to leave things as they are.

And so, in these days of difficulty, we Americans everywhere must and shall choose the path of social justice—the only path that will lead us to a permanent bettering of our civilization, the path that our children must tread and their children must tread, the path of faith, the path of hope and the path of love toward our fellow man.

PART II

First and Second Presidential Terms

(1933–1941)

10.

The Only Thing We Have to Fear Is Fear Itself

First Inaugural Address
Washington, DC, March 4, 1933

After winning the presidency in November 1932, FDR was not inaugurated until March 1933. In the intervening months the Great Depression grew worse. Fear gripped the nation. Roosevelt, however, was determined to rally Americans for the fight ahead. In his first inaugural address he promised action to restore trust and "ancient values," subject corporate and financial activity to federal regulation, and create jobs. Towards those ends, he called on Congress and his fellow Americans to join in the struggle as if they were at war—which to some sounded dangerously authoritarian in view of the rise of fascism in Europe. But he had no dictatorial ambitions. In the course of the now-famous first one hundred days of his presidency, FDR and his New Deal cabinet acted deliberately and quickly with the new Democratic-controlled Congress not simply to make real his political promises, but also to enable Americans to make America all the more democratic.

I am certain that my fellow Americans expect that on my induction into the presidency I will address them with a candor and a decision which the present situation of our nation impels. This is preeminently the time to speak the truth, the whole truth, frankly and boldly. Nor need we shrink from honestly facing conditions in our country today. This great nation will endure as it has endured, will revive and will prosper. So, first of all, let me assert my firm belief that the only thing we have to fear is fear itself—nameless, unreasoning, unjustified terror which paralyzes needed efforts to convert retreat into advance. In every dark hour of our national life a leadership of frankness and vigor has met with that understanding and support of the people themselves which is essential to victory. I am convinced that you will again give that support to leadership in these critical days.

In such a spirit on my part and on yours we face our common difficulties. They concern, thank God, only material things. Values have shrunken to fantastic levels; taxes have risen; our ability to pay has fallen; government of all kinds is faced by serious curtailment of income; the means of exchange are frozen in the currents of trade; the withered leaves of industrial enterprise lie on every side; farmers find no markets for their produce; the savings of many years in thousands of families are gone.

More important, a host of unemployed citizens face the grim problem of existence, and an equally great number toil with little return. Only a foolish optimist can deny the dark realities of the moment.

Yet our distress comes from no failure of substance. We are stricken by no plague of locusts. Compared with the perils which our forefathers conquered because they believed and were not afraid, we have still much to be thankful for. Nature still offers her bounty and human efforts have multiplied it. Plenty is at our doorstep, but a generous use of it languishes in the very sight of the supply. Primarily this is because rulers of the exchange of mankind's goods have failed through their own stubbornness and their own incompetence, have admitted their failure, and have abdicated. Practices of the unscrupulous money changers stand indicted in the court of public opinion, rejected by the hearts and minds of men.

True they have tried, but their efforts have been cast in the pattern of an outworn tradition. Faced by failure of credit they have proposed only the lending of more money. Stripped of the lure of profit by which to induce our people to follow their false leadership, they have resorted to exhortations, pleading tearfully for restored confidence. They know only the rules of a generation of self-seekers. They have no vision, and when there is no vision the people perish.

The money changers have fled from their high seats in the temple of our civilization. We may now restore that temple to the ancient truths. The measure of the restoration lies in the extent to which we apply social values more noble than mere monetary profit.

Happiness lies not in the mere possession of money; it lies in the joy of achievement, in the thrill of creative effort. The joy and moral stimulation of work no longer must be forgotten in the mad chase of evanescent profits. These dark days will be worth all they cost us if they teach us that our true destiny is not to be ministered unto but to minister to ourselves and to our fellow men.

Recognition of the falsity of material wealth as the standard of success goes hand in hand with the abandonment of the false belief that public office and high political position are to be valued only by the standards of pride of place and personal profit; and there must be an end to a conduct in banking and in business which too often has given to a sacred trust the likeness of callous and selfish wrongdoing. Small wonder that confidence languishes, for it thrives only on honesty, on honor, on the sacredness of obligations, on faithful protection, on unselfish performance; without them it cannot live.

Restoration calls, however, not for changes in ethics alone. This nation asks for action, and action now.

Our greatest primary task is to put people to work. This is no unsolvable problem if we face it wisely and courageously. It can be accomplished in part by direct recruiting by the government itself, treating the task as we would treat the emergency of a war, but at the same time, through this employment, accomplishing greatly needed projects to stimulate and reorganize the use of our natural resources.

Hand in hand with this we must frankly recognize the overbalance of population in our industrial centers and, by engaging on a national scale in a redistribution, endeavor to provide a better use of the land for those best fitted for the land. The task can be helped by definite efforts to raise the values of agricultural products and with this the power to purchase the output of our cities. It can be helped by preventing realistically the tragedy of the growing loss through foreclosure of our small homes and our farms. It can be helped by insistence that the federal, state, and local governments act forthwith on the demand that their cost be drastically reduced. It can be helped by the unifying of relief activities which today are often scattered, uneconomical, and unequal. It can be helped by national planning for and supervision of all forms of transportation and of communications and other utilities which have a definitely public character. There are many ways in which it can be helped, but it can never be helped merely by talking about it. We must act and act quickly.

Finally, in our progress toward a resumption of work we require two safeguards against a return of the evils of the old order: there must be a strict supervision of all banking and credits and investments, so that there will be an end to speculation with other people's money; and there must be provision for an adequate but sound currency.

These are the lines of attack. I shall presently urge upon a new Congress, in special session, detailed measures for their fulfillment, and I shall seek the immediate assistance of the several states.

Through this program of action we address ourselves to putting our own national house in order and making income balance outgo. Our international trade relations, though vastly important, are in point of time and necessity secondary to the establishment of a sound national economy. I favor as a practical policy the putting of first things first. I shall spare no effort to restore world trade by international economic readjustment, but the emergency at home cannot wait on that accomplishment.

The basic thought that guides these specific means of national recovery is not narrowly nationalistic. It is the insistence, as a first considerations, upon the interdependence of the various elements in and parts of the United States—a recognition of the old and permanently important manifestation of the American spirit of the pioneer. It is the way to recovery. It is the immediate way. It is the strongest assurance that the recovery will endure.

In the field of world policy I would dedicate this nation to the policy of the good neighbor—the neighbor who resolutely respects himself and, because he does so, respects the rights of others—the neighbor who respects his obligations and respects the sanctity of his agreements in and with a world of neighbors.

If I read the temper of our people correctly, we now realize as we have never realized before our interdependence on each other; that we cannot merely take but we must give as well; that if we are to go forward, we must move as a trained and loyal army willing to sacrifice for the good of a common discipline, because without such discipline no progress is made, no leadership becomes effective. We are, I know, ready and willing to submit our lives and property to such discipline, because it makes possible a leadership which aims at a larger good. This I propose to offer, pledging that the larger purposes will bind upon us all as a sacred obligation with a unity of duty hitherto evoked only in time of armed strife.

With this pledge taken, I assume unhesitatingly the leadership of this great army of our people dedicated to a disciplined attack upon our common problems.

Action in this image and to this end is feasible under the form of government which we have inherited from our ancestors. Our Constitution is so simple and practical that it is possible always to meet extraordinary needs by changes in emphasis and arrangement without loss of essential form. That is why our constitutional system has proved itself the most superbly enduring political mechanism the modern world has produced. It has met every stress of vast expansion of territory, of foreign wars, of bitter internal strife, of world relations.

It is to be hoped that the normal balance of executive and legislative authority may be wholly adequate to meet the unprecedented task before us. But it may be that an unprecedented demand and need for undelayed action may call for temporary departure from that normal balance of public procedure.

I am prepared under my constitutional duty to recommend the measures that a stricken nation in the midst of a stricken world may require. These measures, or such other measures as the Congress may build out of its experience and wisdom, I shall seek, within my constitutional authority, to bring to speedy adoption.

But in the event that the Congress shall fail to take one of these two courses, and in the event that the national emergency is still critical, I shall not evade the clear course of duty that will then confront me. I shall ask the Congress for the one remaining instrument to meet the crisis—broad executive power to wage a war against the emergency, as great as the power that would be given to me if we were in fact invaded by a foreign foe.

For the trust reposed in me I will return the courage and the devotion that befit the time. I can do no less.

We face the arduous days that lie before us in the warm courage of national unity; with the clear consciousness of seeking old and precious moral values; with the clean satisfaction that comes from the stern performance of duty by old and young alike. We aim at the assurance of a rounded and permanent national life.

We do not distrust the future of essential democracy. The people of the United States have not failed. In their need they have registered a mandate that they want direct, vigorous action. They have asked for discipline and direction under leadership. They have made me the present instrument of their wishes. In the spirit of the gift I take it.

In this dedication of a nation we humbly ask the blessing of God. May He protect each and every one of us. May He guide me in the days to come.

11.

To Put People Back to Work

Presidential Statement on the National Industrial Recovery Act
Washington, DC, June 16, 1933

The National Industrial Recovery Act (NIRA) was intended to revive industrial and commercial activity, raise workers' purchasing power, and promote cooperation between business and labor. It not only suspended antitrust laws, established industry-wide councils of corporate leaders that were to issue codes regulating production, prices, and wages, and created labor and consumer advisory boards, but also stipulated that workers had a right to organize and bargain collectively—which they would soon do in the millions. Notably, while the Act included the setting of a "minimum wage" in industry, FDR himself stated on signing it that "It seems to me to be equally plain that no business which depends for existence on paying less than living wages to its workers has any right to continue in this country."

The law I have just signed was passed to put people back to work, to let them buy more of the products of farms and factories and start our business at a living rate again. This task is in two stages; first, to get many hundreds of thousands of the unemployed back on the payroll by snowfall and, second, to plan for a better future for the longer pull. While we shall not neglect the second, the first stage is an emergency job. It has the right of way.

The second part of the Act gives employment through a vast program of public works. Our studies show that we should be able to hire many men at once and to step up to about a million new jobs by October first, and a much greater number later. We must put at the head of our list those works which are fully ready to start now. Our first purpose is to create employment as fast as we can, but we should not pour money into unproved projects.

We have worked out our plans for action. Some of the work will start tomorrow . . .

In my Inaugural I laid down the simple proposition that nobody is going to starve in this country. It seems to me to be equally plain that no business which depends for existence on paying less than living wages to its workers has any right to continue in this country. By business I mean the whole of commerce as well as the whole of industry; by workers I mean all workers, the white-collar class as well as the men in overalls; and by living wages I mean more than a bare subsistence level—I mean the wages of decent living.

Throughout industry, the change from starvation wages and starvation employment to living wages and sustained employment can, in large part, be made by an industrial covenant to which all employers shall subscribe. It is greatly to their interest to do this because decent living, widely spread among our 125,000,000 people, eventually means the opening up to industry of the richest market which the world has known. It is the only way to utilize the so-called excess capacity of our industrial plants. This is the principle that makes this one of the most important laws that ever has come from Congress because, before the passage of this Act, no such industrial covenant was possible.

On this idea, the first part of the Act proposes to our industry a great spontaneous cooperation to put millions of men back in their regular jobs this summer. The idea is simply for employers to hire more men to do the existing work by reducing the work-hours of each man's week and at the same time paying a living wage for the shorter week.

No employer and no group of less than all employers in a single trade could do this alone and continue to live in business competition. But if all employers in each trade now band themselves faithfully in these modern guilds—without exception—and agree to act together and at once, none will be hurt and millions of workers, so long deprived of the right to earn their bread in the sweat of their labor, can raise their heads again. The challenge of this law is whether we can sink selfish interest and present a solid front against a common peril.

It is a challenge to industry which has long insisted that, given the right to act in unison, it could do much for the general good which has hitherto been unlawful. From today it has that right. . . .

This law is also a challenge to labor. Workers, too, are here given a new charter of rights long sought and hitherto denied. But they know that the first move expected by the nation is a great cooperation of all employers, by one single mass-action, to improve the case of workers on a scale never attempted in any nation. Industries can do this only if they have the support of the whole public and especially of their own workers. This is not a law to foment discord and it will not be executed as such. This is a time for mutual confidence and help and we can safely rely on the sense of fair play among all Americans to assure every industry which now moves forward promptly in this united drive against depression that its workers will be with it to a man.

It is, further, a challenge to administration. We are relaxing some of the safeguards of the anti-trust laws. The public must be protected against the abuses that led to their enactment, and to this end, we are putting in place of old principles of unchecked competition some new government controls. They must, above all, be impartial and just. Their purpose is to free business, not to shackle it; and no man who stands on the constructive, forward-looking side of his industry has anything to fear from them. To such men the opportunities for individual initiative will open more amply than ever. Let me make it clear, however, that the anti-trust laws still stand firmly against monopolies that restrain trade and price fixing which allows inordinate profits or unfairly high prices. . . .

Finally, this law is a challenge to our whole people. There is no power in America that can force against the public will such action as we require. But there is no group in America that can withstand the force of an aroused public opinion. This great cooperation can succeed only if those who bravely go forward to restore jobs have aggressive public support and those who lag are made to feel the full weight of public disapproval.

As to the machinery, we shall use the practical way of accomplishing what we are setting out to do. When a trade association has a code ready to submit and the association has qualified as truly representative, and after reasonable notice has been issued to all concerned, a public hearing will be held by the Administrator or a deputy. A Labor Advisory Board appointed by the Secretary of Labor will be responsible that every affected labor group, whether organized or unorganized, is fully and adequately represented in an advisory capacity and any interested labor group will be entitled to be heard through representatives of its own choosing. An Industrial Advisory Board appointed by the Secretary of Commerce will be responsible that every affected industrial group is fully and adequately represented in an advisory capacity and any interested industrial group will be entitled to be heard through representatives of its own choosing. A Consumers Advisory Board will be responsible that the interests of the consuming public will be represented and every reasonable opportunity will be given to any group or class who may be affected directly or indirectly to present their views.

At the conclusion of these hearings and after the most careful scrutiny by a competent economic staff, the Administrator will present the subject to me for my action under the law. . . .

Between these twin efforts—public works and industrial reemployment—it is not too much to expect that a great many men and women can be taken from the ranks of the unemployed before winter comes. It is the most important attempt of this kind in history. As in the great crisis of the World War, it puts a whole people to the simple but vital test: "Must we go on in many groping, disorganized, separate units to defeat or shall we move as one great team to victory?"

12.

You Young Men and Women Have a Duty to Your Whole Community

Speech at Washington College
Chestertown, Maryland, October 21, 1933

Receiving an honorary degree from Washington College, Roosevelt encour-
aged the students at the school to recognize the duty they had to apply
the knowledge they were acquiring to addressing the needs of the nation.
Moreover, he spoke of the imperative of creating a "wider . . . distribution
of wealth" and of the need to make education itself more widely available—
both of which would become regular themes of his presidency.

. . . . You young men and young women who are attending this College, like the young men and young women who are attending all the colleges throughout the land, have a duty to your whole community. I often think of the words of a very elderly gentleman, President Eliot of Harvard, who, in many ways, was a revolutionist in educational circles. We were talking about the value of the educated people of the country to the country, and he made this remark, which I have always remembered: "If the ballot of the United States were limited to the holders of college degrees, the country would probably last about two years." And then he went on making the obvious point that if the governing of the United States were confined to one partic- ular class of the community, whether they have the privilege of wealth or of education, something would be bound to go wrong, because of the very sim- ple fact that there would be representation of only a minority of the people.

The wider we can have a distribution of wealth in the proper sense of that term, the more we can make it possible for every man, woman, and child throughout the land to have the necessities; and when they find themselves in such shape that they do not have to lie awake nights won- dering where the food for the morrow is coming from, then we shall have the kind of security which means so much to the progress and the spirit of the country.

In the same way, if we could provide in the nation for an adequate education for everybody, the spirit of the country would be vastly safeguarded. It is.in this spirit that we encourage and foster the institutions of this nation. And throughout the land, it is in this spirit that we are seeking, in times of depression, to prevent further attack on our educational system, which is building up the possibilities of this education to every boy and girl. In the last analysis we need people who have had a chance to look not just at the history of things in the past, but to look also into the application of that history to the problems of the moment and future. It is that thought which leads to an ideal of education.

I remember that when I was a boy in school in Massachusetts, Bishop Phillips Brooks made to my class a remark I shall never forget. He said: "You boys will be good citizens just as long as you remember your boyhood ideals." Those young ideals are just as true today as they were then. The ideals of young people are, on the whole, pretty fine and sound from the point of view of principle. Today they are making many changes in the methods, and many changes in the machinery of life, not just of government but of all human relationships, just as they will continue to make them; for a great many changes of government and human relationships are perfectly proper. But at the same time, the old-fashioned boyhood ideals, the old-fashioned principles, are going to keep the country going.

Every man and woman with an education has a twofold duty to perform. The first is to apply that education intelligently to problems of the moment; and the second is to obtain and maintain contact with and understanding of the average citizens of their own country. We have accomplished much, my friends, I think a great deal, in the last few months. Some countries which have dictators have laid down four-, five- and ten-year programs. I believe that in this country, which has not a dictatorship, we can move further toward our goal in a shorter space of time without giving it a definite number of years.

13.

Relief, Recovery, Reform, and Reconstruction

A Fireside Chat
June 28, 1934

In this Fireside Chat, Roosevelt spoke of his administration's determination to pursue not only "relief and recovery," but also "reform and reconstruction." He also began to project the establishment of a national system of "social insurance." But in the face of ongoing political attacks from the political right and the corporate rich, he necessarily warned Americans to not allow themselves to be fooled by conservatives and reactionaries who were trying to pejoratively brand such initiatives as "regimentation, Fascism, or Communism."

It has been several months since I have talked with you concerning the problems of government. Since January, those of us in whom you have vested responsibility have been engaged in the fulfillment of plans and policies which had been widely discussed in previous months. It seemed to us our duty not only to make the right path clear, but also to tread that path.

As we review the achievements of this session of the Seventy-third Congress, it is made increasingly clear that its task was essentially that of completing and fortifying the work it had begun in March 1933. . . .

In the consistent development of our previous efforts toward the saving and safeguarding of our national life, I have continued to recognize three related steps. The first was relief, because the primary concern of any government dominated by the humane ideals of democracy is the simple principle that in a land of vast resources no one should be permitted to starve. Relief was and continues to be our first consideration. It calls for large expenditures and will continue in modified form to do so for a long time to come. . . .

The second step was recovery, and it is sufficient for me to ask each and every one of you to compare the situation in agriculture and in industry today with what it was fifteen months ago.

At the same time we have recognized the necessity of reform and reconstruction—reform because much of our trouble today and in the past few years has been due to a lack of understanding of the elementary principles of justice and fairness by those in whom leadership in business and finance was placed—reconstruction because new conditions in our economic life as well as old but neglected conditions had to be corrected.

Substantial gains well known to all of you have justified our course. I could cite statistics to you as unanswerable measures of our national progress. . . .

But the simplest way for each of you to judge recovery lies in the plain facts of your own individual situation. Are you better off than you were last year? Are your debts less burdensome? Is your bank account more secure? Are your working conditions better? Is your faith in your own individual future more firmly grounded?

Have you lost any of your rights or liberty or constitutional freedom of action and choice? Turn to the Bill of Rights of the Constitution, which I have solemnly sworn to maintain and under which your freedom rests secure. Read each provision of that Bill of Rights and ask yourself whether you personally have suffered the impairment of a single jot of these great assurances. I have no question in my mind as to what your answer will be. The record is written in the experiences of your own personal lives. . . .

In the working out of a great national program which seeks the primary good of the greater number, it is true that the toes of some people are being stepped on and are going to be stepped on. But these toes belong to the comparative few who seek to retain or to gain position or riches or both by some shortcut which is harmful to the greater good. . . .

But, in addition to this our immediate task, we must still look to the larger future. I have pointed out to the Congress that we are seeking to find the way once more to well-known, long-established but to some degree forgotten ideals and values. We seek the security of the men, women, and children of the nation.

That security involves added means of providing better homes for the people of the nation. That is the first principle of our future program.

The second is to plan the use of land and water resources of this country to the end that the means of livelihood of our citizens may be more adequate to meet their daily needs.

And, finally, the third principle is to use the agencies of government to assist in the establishment of means to provide sound and adequate protection against the vicissitudes of modern life—in other words, social insurance.

Later in the year I hope to talk with you more fully about these plans.

A few timid people, who fear progress, will try to give you new and strange names for what we are doing. Sometimes they will call it "Fascism," sometimes "Communism," sometimes "Regimentation," sometimes "Socialism." But in so doing, they are trying to make very complex and theoretical something that is really very simple and very practical.

I believe in practical explanations and in practical policies. I believe that what we are doing today is a necessary fulfillment of what Americans have always been doing—a fulfillment of old and tested American ideals.

14.

The Average Man Waged a Long and Bitter Fight for His Rights

Open-Air Address in Green Bay
Green Bay, Wisconsin, August 9, 1934

With the November midterm elections on the horizon, FDR delivered an open-air speech to the working people of Green Bay in which he spoke historically of the struggles of working people to secure the rights and securities denied them in Europe and to create a prosperous and democratic Wisconsin and America. To those in attendance it must surely have been apparent that he was expressing his endorsement of the workers on strike against the Kohler Company, located just sixty miles south of Green Bay, who were demanding that the company recognize their right to organize an independent labor union and bargain collectively. In fact, only weeks before, police had fired on and used tear gas against the strikers, killing two workers and injuring dozens of others.

Governor Schmedeman, Mr. Mayor, my friends:

This is an inspiration to be here today. This is a wonderful setting on the shores of the Bay and I am glad to take part in this commemoration of the landing in Green Bay of the man who can truly be called the first white pioneer of this part of the United States. Over all the years, as your distinguished representative in Congress has suggested, the purposes of the men and women who established civilization in Wisconsin and in the Northwest were the same as those that stimulated the earlier settlers of the Atlantic Seaboard. Men everywhere throughout Europe—your ancestors and mine—had suffered from the imperfect and often unjust governments of their home land, and they were driven by deep desire to find not only security, but also enlarged opportunity for themselves and their children. It is true that the new population flowing into our new lands was a mixed population, differing often in language, in external customs, and in habits of thought. But in one thing they were alike. They shared a deep purpose to rid themselves forever of the jealousies, the prejudices, the intrigues, and the violence, whether internal or external, that disturbed their lives on the other side of the ocean.

Yes, they sought a life that was less fettered by the exploitations of self-ish men, set up under governments that were not free. They sought a wider opportunity for the average man.

Having achieved that initial adventure of migrating to new homes, they moved forward to the further adventure of establishing forms of government and methods of operating these forms of government that might assure them the things they sought. They believed that men, out of their intelligence and their self-discipline, could create and use forms of government that would not enslave the human spirit, but free it and nourish it throughout the generations. They did not fear government, because they knew that government in the new world was their own.

I do not need to tell you that here in Wisconsin they built a state destined for extraordinary achievements. They set up institutions to enforce law and order, to care for the unfortunate, to promote the arts of industry and agriculture. They built a university and school system as enlightened as any that the world affords. They set up against all selfish private interests the organized authority of the people themselves through the state. They transformed utilities into public servants instead of private means of exploitation.

People know also that the average man in Wisconsin waged a long and bitter fight for his rights. Here, and in the nation as a whole, in the nation at large, this battle has been two-fold.

It has been a fight against nature. From the time that the settlers started to clear the land until now, they have been compelled to assert the power of their brains and courage over the blind powers of the wind and the sun and the soil. They have paid no heed to the reactionaries who would tell them that mankind must stand impotent before the forces of nature. Year after year, as science progressed and mastery of the mysteries of the physical universe increased, man has been turning nature, once his hard master, into useful servitude.

That is why, on this trip across the northern part of this continent, I have been so moved by the distressing effects of a widespread drought, and at the same time so strengthened in my belief that science and cooperation can do much from now on to undo the mistakes that men have made in the past and to aid the good forces of nature and the good impulses of men instead of fighting against them.

Yes, we are but carrying forward the fundamentals behind the pioneering spirit of the fathers when we apply the pioneering methods to the better use of vast land and water resources—what God has given us to use as trustees not only for ourselves but for future generations.

But man has been fighting also against those forces which disregard human cooperation and human rights in seeking that kind of individual profit which is gained at the expense of his fellows.

It is just as hard to achieve harmonious and cooperative action among human beings as it is to conquer the forces of nature. Only through the submerging of individual desires into unselfish and practical cooperation can civilization grow.

In the great national movement that culminated over a year ago, people joined with enthusiasm. They lent hand and voice to the common cause, irrespective of many older political traditions. They saw the dawn of a new day. They were on the march; they were coming back into the possession of their own home land.

As the humble instruments of their vision and their power, those of us who were chosen to serve them in 1932 turned to the great task.

In one year and five months, the people of the United States have received at least a partial answer to their demands for action; and neither the demand nor the action has reached the end of the road.

But, my friends, action may be delayed by two types of individuals. Let me cite examples: First, there is the man whose objectives are wholly right and wholly progressive but who declines to cooperate or even to discuss methods of arriving at the objectives because he insists on his own methods and nobody's else.

The other type to which I refer is the kind of individual who demands some message to the people of the United States that will restore what he calls "confidence." When I hear this I cannot help but remember the pleas that were made by government and certain types of so-called "big business" all through the years 1930, 1931, and 1932, that the only thing lacking in the United States was confidence. . . .

The people of the United States will not restore that ancient order. There is no lack of confidence on the part of those business men, farmers and workers who clearly read the signs of the times. Sound economic improvement comes from the improved conditions of the whole population and not a small fraction thereof.

Those who would measure confidence in this country in the future must look first to the average citizen.

15.

I Place the Security of the Men, Women, and Children of This Nation First

Annual Message to Congress
Washington, DC, January 4, 1935

In this Annual Message to Congress, Roosevelt projected a fresh round of initiatives that historians would come to call the Second New Deal. The Democrats had significantly increased their numbers in Congress in November 1934, which would enable Roosevelt to not only create new programs to battle the Great Depression, most notably the Works Progress Administration (WPA), but also both to move in favor of establishing his envisioned Social Security program and to finally endorse the passage of the National Labor Relations Act (NLRA)—aka the "Wagner Act," after its author, New York Senator Robert F. Wagner—which empowered the federal government to guarantee workers the right to organize independent labor unions and bargain collectively.

Mr. President, Mr. Speaker, Members of the Senate and of the House of Representatives:

The Constitution wisely provides that the Chief Executive shall report to the Congress on the state of the Union, for through you, the chosen legislative representatives, our citizens everywhere may fairly judge the progress of our governing. I am confident that today, in the light of the events of the past two years, you do not consider it merely a trite phrase when I tell you that I am truly glad to greet you and that I look forward to common counsel, to useful cooperation, and to genuine friendships between us.

We have undertaken a new order of things; yet we progress to it under the framework and in the spirit and intent of the American Constitution. We have proceeded throughout the nation a measurable distance on the road toward this new order.

Materially, I can report to you substantial benefits to our agricultural population, increased industrial activity, and profits to our merchants. Of equal moment, there is evident a restoration of that spirit of confidence and faith which marks the American character. Let him, who, for speculative profit or partisan purpose, without just warrant would seek to disturb or dispel this assurance, take heed before he assumes responsibility for any act which slows our onward steps.

Throughout the world, change is the order of the day. In every nation economic problems, long in the making, have brought crises of many kinds for which the masters of old practice and theory were unprepared. In most nations social justice, no longer a distant ideal, has become a definite goal, and ancient governments are beginning to heed the call.

Thus, the American people do not stand alone in the world in their desire for change. We seek it through tested liberal traditions, through processes which retain all of the deep essentials of that republican form of representative government first given to a troubled world by the United States.

As the various parts in the program begun in the Extraordinary Session of the Seventy-third Congress shape themselves in practical administration, the unity of our program reveals itself to the nation. The outlines of the new economic order, rising from the disintegration of the old, are apparent. We test what we have done as our measures take root in the living texture of life. We see where we have built wisely and where we can do still better.

The attempt to make a distinction between recovery and reform is a narrowly conceived effort to substitute the appearance of reality for reality itself. When a man is convalescing from illness, wisdom dictates not only cure of the symptoms, but also removal of their cause.

It is important to recognize that while we seek to outlaw specific abuses, the American objective of today has an infinitely deeper, finer, and more lasting purpose than mere repression. Thinking people in almost every country of the world have come to realize certain fundamental difficulties with which civilization must reckon. Rapid changes—the machine age, the advent of universal and rapid communication, and many other new factors—have brought new problems. Succeeding generations have attempted to keep pace by reforming in piecemeal fashion this or that attendant abuse. As a result, evils overlap and reform becomes confused and frustrated. We lose sight, from time to time, of our ultimate human objectives.

Let us, for a moment, strip from our simple purpose the confusion that results from a multiplicity of detail and from millions of written and spoken words.

We find our population suffering from old inequalities, little changed by vast sporadic remedies. In spite of our efforts and in spite of our talk, we have not weeded out the over privileged and we have not effectively lifted up the underprivileged. Both of these manifestations of injustice have retarded happiness. No wise man has any intention of destroying what is known as the profit motive; because by the profit motive we mean the right by work to earn a decent livelihood for ourselves and for our families.

We have, however, a clear mandate from the people, that Americans must forswear that conception of the acquisition of wealth which, through excessive profits, creates undue private power over private affairs and, to our misfortune, over public affairs as well. In building toward this end we do not destroy ambition, nor do we seek to divide our wealth into equal shares on stated occasions. We continue to recognize the greater ability of some to earn more than others. But we do assert that the ambition of the individual to obtain for him and his a proper security, a reasonable leisure, and a decent living throughout life, is an ambition to be preferred to the appetite for great wealth and great power.

I recall to your attention my message to the Congress last June in which I said: "among our objectives I place the security of the men, women, and children of the nation first." That remains our first and continuing task; and in a very real sense every major legislative enactment of this Congress should be a component part of it.

In defining immediate factors which enter into our quest, I have spoken to the Congress and the people of three great divisions:

1. The security of a livelihood through the better use of the national resources of the land in which we live.
2. The security against the major hazards and vicissitudes of life.
3. The security of decent homes.

I am now ready to submit to the Congress a broad program designed ultimately to establish all three of these factors of security —a program which because of many lost years will take many future years to fulfill.

A study of our national resources, more comprehensive than any previously made, shows the vast amount of necessary and practicable work which needs to be done for the development and preservation of our natural wealth for the enjoyment and advantage of our people in generations to come. The sound use of land and water is far more comprehensive than the mere planting of trees, building of dams, distributing of electricity, or retirement of sub-marginal land. It recognizes that stranded populations, either in the country or the city, cannot have security under the conditions that now surround them.

To this end we are ready to begin to meet this problem—the intelligent care of population throughout our nation, in accordance with an intelligent distribution of the means of livelihood for that population. A definite program for putting people to work, of which I shall speak in a moment, is a component part of this greater program of security of livelihood through the better use of our national resources.

Closely related to the broad problem of livelihood is that of security against the major hazards of life. Here also, a comprehensive survey of what has been attempted or accomplished in many nations and in many states proves to me that the time has come for action by the national government. I shall send to you, in a few days, definite recommendations based on these studies. These recommendations will cover the broad subjects of unemployment insurance and old age insurance, of benefits for children, for others, for the handicapped, for maternity care, and for other aspects of dependency and illness where a beginning can now be made.

The third factor—better homes for our people—has also been the subject of experimentation and study. Here, too, the first practical steps can be made through the proposals which I shall suggest in relation to giving work to the unemployed.

Whatever we plan and whatever we do should be in the light of these three clear objectives of security. We cannot afford to lose valuable time in haphazard public policies which cannot find a place in the broad outlines of these major purposes. In that spirit I come to an immediate issue made for us by hard and inescapable circumstance—the task of putting people to work. In the spring of 1933 the issue of destitution seemed to stand apart; today, in the light of our experience and our new national policy, we find we can put people to work in ways which conform to, initiate, and carry forward the broad principles of that policy.

The first objectives of emergency legislation of 1933 were to relieve destitution, to make it possible for industry to operate in a more rational and orderly fashion, and to put behind industrial recovery the impulse of large expenditures in government undertakings. The purpose of the National Industrial Recovery Act to provide work for more people succeeded in a substantial manner within the first few months of its life, and the Act has continued to maintain employment gains and greatly improved working conditions in industry.

The program of public works provided for in the Recovery Act launched the federal government into a task for which there was little time to make preparation and little American experience to follow. Great employment has been given and is being given by these works.

More than two billions of dollars have also been expended in direct relief to the destitute. Local agencies of necessity determined the recipients of this form of relief. With inevitable exceptions the funds were spent by them with reasonable efficiency and as a result actual want of food and clothing in the great majority of cases has been overcome.

But the stark fact before us is that great numbers still remain unemployed.

A large proportion of these unemployed and their dependents have been forced on the relief rolls. The burden on the federal government has grown with great rapidity. We have here a human as well as an economic problem. When humane considerations are concerned, Americans give them precedence. The lessons of history, confirmed by the evidence immediately before me, show conclusively that continued dependence upon relief induces a spiritual and moral disintegration fundamentally destructive to the national fiber. To dole out relief in this way is to administer a narcotic, a subtle destroyer of the human spirit. It is inimical to the dictates of sound policy. It is in violation of the traditions of America. Work must be found for able-bodied but destitute workers.

The federal government must and shall quit this business of relief.

I am not willing that the vitality of our people be further sapped by the giving of cash, of market baskets, of a few hours of weekly work cutting grass, raking leaves, or picking up papers in the public parks. We must preserve not only the bodies of the unemployed from destitution but also their self-respect, their self-reliance and courage and determination. This decision brings me to the problem of what the government should do with approximately five million unemployed now on the relief rolls.

About one million and a half of these belong to the group which in the past was dependent upon local welfare efforts. Most of them are unable for one reason or another to maintain themselves independently—for the most part, through no fault of their own. Such people, in the days before the Great Depression, were cared for by local efforts—by states, by counties, by towns, by cities, by churches, and by private welfare agencies. It is my thought that in the future they must be cared for as they were before. I stand ready through my own personal efforts, and through the public influence of the office that I hold, to help these local agencies to get the means necessary to assume this burden.

The security legislation which I shall propose to the Congress will, I am confident, be of assistance to local effort in the care of this type of cases. Local responsibility can and will be resumed, for, after all, common sense tells us that the wealth necessary for this task existed and still exists in the local community, and the dictates of sound administration require that this responsibility be in the first instance a local one.

There are, however, an additional three and one half million employable people who are on relief. With them the problem is different and the responsibility is different. This group was the victim of a nationwide depression caused by conditions which were not local but national. The federal government is the only governmental agency with sufficient power and credit to meet this situation. We have assumed this task and we shall not shrink from it in the future. It is a duty dictated by every intelligent consideration of national policy to ask you to make it possible for the United States to give employment to all of these three and one half million employable people now on relief, pending their absorption in a rising tide of private employment.

It is my thought that with the exception of certain of the normal public building operations of the government, all emergency public works shall be united in a single new and greatly enlarged plan.

With the establishment of this new system we can supersede the Federal Emergency Relief Administration with a coordinated authority which will be charged with the orderly liquidation of our present relief activities and the substitution of a national chart for the giving of work. . . .

Ever since the adjournment of the Seventy-third Congress, the administration has been studying from every angle the possibility and the practicability of new forms of employment. As a result of these studies I have arrived at certain very definite convictions as to the amount of money that will be necessary for the sort of public projects that I have described. I shall submit these figures in my budget message. I assure you now they will be within the sound credit of the government.

The work itself will cover a wide field including clearance of slums, which for adequate reasons cannot be undertaken by private capital; in rural housing of several kinds, where, again, private capital is unable to function; in rural electrification; in the reforestation of the great watersheds of the nation; in an intensified program to prevent soil erosion and to reclaim blighted areas; in improving existing road systems and in constructing national highways designed to handle modern traffic; in the elimination of grade crossings; in the extension and enlargement of the successful work of the Civilian Conservation Corps; in non-federal works, mostly self-liquidating and highly useful to local divisions of government; and on many other projects which the nation needs and cannot afford to neglect.

This is the method which I propose to you in order that we may better meet this present-day problem of unemployment. Its greatest advantage is that it fits logically and usefully into the long-range permanent policy of providing the three types of security which constitute as a whole an American plan for the betterment of the future of the American people ...

The ledger of the past year shows many more gains than losses. Let us not forget that, in addition to saving millions from utter destitution, child labor has been for the moment outlawed, thousands of homes saved to their owners, and most important of all, the morale of the nation has been restored. Viewing the year 1934 as a whole, you and I can agree that we have a generous measure of reasons for giving thanks.

It is not empty optimism that moves me to a strong hope in the coming year. We can, if we will, make 1935 a genuine period of good feeling, sustained by a sense of purposeful progress. Beyond the material recovery, I sense a spiritual recovery as well. The people of America are turning as never before to those permanent values that are not limited to the physical objectives of life. There are growing signs of this on every hand. In the face of these spiritual impulses we are sensible of the Divine Providence to which nations turn now, as always, for guidance and fostering care.

16.

I Promised to Submit a Definite Program of Action

Message to Congress on Social Security
January 17, 1935

Following up quickly on his Annual Message, FDR formally proposed a social security system to include unemployment benefits, old-age benefits, and aid to families with dependent children.

To the Congress:

... In my annual message to you I promised to submit a definite program of action [to secure "men, women, and children of the nation against certain hazards and vicissitudes of life"]. This I do in the form of a report to me by a Committee on Economic Security, appointed by me for the purpose of surveying the field and of recommending the basis of legislation.

I am gratified with the work of this Committee and of those who have helped it.... All of those who participated in this notable task of planning this major legislative proposal are ready and willing, at any time, to consult with and assist in any way the appropriate congressional committees and members, with respect to detailed aspects....

The detailed report of the Committee sets forth a series of proposals that will appeal to the sound sense of the American people. It has not attempted the impossible, nor has it failed to exercise sound caution and consideration of all of the factors concerned: the national credit, the rights and responsibilities of states, the capacity of industry to assume financial responsibilities, and the fundamental necessity of proceeding in a manner that will merit the enthusiastic support of citizens of all sorts.

It is overwhelmingly important to avoid any danger of permanently discrediting the sound and necessary policy of federal legislation for economic security by attempting to apply it on too ambitious a scale before actual experience has provided guidance for the permanently safe direction of such efforts. The place of such a fundamental in our future civilization is too precious to be jeopardized now by extravagant action. It is a sound idea—a sound ideal. Most of the other advanced countries of the world have already adopted it and their experience affords the knowledge that social insurance can be made a sound and workable project.

Three principles should be observed in legislation on this subject. First, the system adopted, except for the money necessary to initiate it, should be self-sustaining in the sense that funds for the payment of insurance benefits should not come from the proceeds of general taxation. Second, excepting in old-age insurance, actual management should be left to the States subject to standards established by the federal government. Third, sound financial management of the funds and the reserves, and protection of the credit structure of the nation should be assured by retaining federal control over all funds through trustees in the Treasury of the United States.

At this time, I recommend the following types of legislation looking to economic security:

1. Unemployment compensation.
2. Old-age benefits, including compulsory and voluntary annuities.
3. Federal aid to dependent children through grants to states for the support of existing mothers' pension systems and for services for the protection and care of homeless, neglected, dependent, and crippled children.
4. Additional federal aid to state and local public-health agencies and the strengthening of the Federal Public Health Service. I am not at this time recommending the adoption of so-called "health insurance," although groups representing the medical profession are cooperating with the federal government in the further study of the subject and definite progress is being made. . . .

The establishment of sound means toward a greater future economic security of the American people is dictated by a prudent consideration of the hazards involved in our national life. No one can guarantee this country against the dangers of future depressions, but we can reduce these dangers. We can eliminate many of the factors that cause economic depressions, and we can provide the means of mitigating their results. This plan for economic security is at once a measure of prevention and a method of alleviation.

We pay now for the dreadful consequence of economic insecurity—and dearly. This plan presents a more equitable and infinitely less expensive means of meeting these costs. We cannot afford to neglect the plain duty before us. I strongly recommend action to attain the objectives sought in this report.

17.

Our Revenue Laws Have Operated to the Unfair Advantage of the Few

Message to Congress on Tax Revision
June 19, 1935

Roosevelt called on Congress to raise taxes on the rich and on corporations. He did not equivocate as to why it was necessary to do so. He stated clearly that the concentration of wealth and economic power "is as inconsistent with the ideals of this generation as inherited political power was inconsistent with the ideals of the generation which established our government."

To the Congress:

As the fiscal year draws to its close it becomes our duty to consider the broad question of tax methods and policies. I wish to acknowledge the timely efforts of the Congress to lay the basis, through its committees, for administrative improvements, by careful study of the revenue systems of our own and of other countries. These studies have made it very clear that we need to simplify and clarify our revenue laws. . . .

On the basis of these studies and of other studies conducted by officials of the Treasury, I am able to make a number of suggestions of important changes in our policy of taxation. These are based on the broad principle that if a government is to be prudent its taxes must produce ample revenues without discouraging enterprise; and if it is to be just it must distribute the burden of taxes equitably. I do not believe that our present system of taxation completely meets this test. Our revenue laws have operated in many ways to the unfair advantage of the few, and they have done little to prevent an unjust concentration of wealth and economic power.

With the enactment of the Income Tax Law of 1913, the federal government began to apply effectively the widely accepted principle that taxes should be levied in proportion to ability to pay and in proportion to the benefits received. Income was wisely chosen as the measure of benefits and of ability to pay. This was, and still is, a wholesome guide for national policy. It should be retained as the governing principle of federal taxation. The use of other forms of taxes is often justifiable, particularly for temporary periods; but taxation according to income is the most effective instrument yet devised to obtain just contribution from those best able to bear it and to avoid placing onerous burdens upon the mass of our people.

The movement toward progressive taxation of wealth and of income has accompanied the growing diversification and interrelation of effort which marks our industrial society. Wealth in the modern world does not come merely from individual effort; it results from a combination of individual effort and of the manifold uses to which the community puts that effort. The individual does not create the product of his industry with his own hands; he utilizes the many processes and forces of mass production to meet the demands of a national and international market.

Therefore, in spite of the great importance in our national life of the efforts and ingenuity of unusual individuals, the people in the mass have inevitably helped to make large fortunes possible. Without mass cooperation great accumulations of wealth would be impossible save by unhealthy speculation. . . .

I

My first proposal, in line with this broad policy, has to do with inheritances and gifts. The transmission from generation to generation of vast fortunes by will, inheritance, or gift is not consistent with the ideals and sentiments of the American people.

The desire to provide security for oneself and one's family is natural and wholesome, but it is adequately served by a reasonable inheritance. Great accumulations of wealth cannot be justified on the basis of personal and family security. In the last analysis such accumulations amount to the perpetuation of great and undesirable concentration of control in a relatively few individuals over the employment and welfare of many, many others.

Such inherited economic power is as inconsistent with the ideals of this generation as inherited political power was inconsistent with the ideals of the generation which established our government.

Creative enterprise is not stimulated by vast inheritances. They bless neither those who bequeath nor those who receive. . . .

A tax upon inherited economic power is a tax upon static wealth, not upon that dynamic wealth which makes for the healthy diffusion of economic good.

Those who argue for the benefits secured to society by great fortunes invested in great businesses should note that such a tax does not affect the essential benefits that remain after the death of the creator of such a business. The mechanism of production that he created remains. The benefits of corporate organization remain. The advantages of pooling many investments in one enterprise remain. Governmental privileges such as patents remain. All that are gone are the initiative, energy, and genius of the creator—and death has taken these away.

I recommend, therefore, that in addition to the present estate taxes, there should be levied an inheritance, succession, and legacy tax in respect to all very large amounts received by any one legatee or beneficiary; and to prevent, so far as possible, evasions of this tax, I recommend further the imposition of gift taxes suited to this end. . . .

II

The disturbing effects upon our national life that come from great inheritances of wealth and power can in the future be reduced, not only through the method I have just described, but through a definite increase in the taxes now levied upon very great individual net incomes.

To illustrate: The application of the principle of a graduated tax now stops at $1,000,000 of annual income. In other words, while the rate for a man with a $6,000 income is double the rate for one with a $4,000 income, a man having a $5,000,000 annual income pays at the same rate as one whose income is $1,000,000.

Social unrest and a deepening sense of unfairness are dangers to our national life which we must minimize by rigorous methods. People know that vast personal incomes come not only through the effort or ability or luck of those who receive them, but also because of the opportunities for advantage which government itself contributes. Therefore, the duty rests upon the government to restrict such incomes by very high taxes.

III

In the modern world scientific invention and mass production have brought many things within the reach of the average man which in an earlier age were available to few. With large-scale enterprise has come the great corporation drawing its resources from widely diversified activities and from a numerous group of investors. The community has profited in those cases in which large-scale production has resulted in substantial economies and lower prices.

The advantages and the protections conferred upon corporations by government increase in value as the size of the corporation increases. Some of these advantages are granted by the state which conferred a charter upon the corporation; others are granted by other states which, as a matter of grace, allow the corporation to do local business within their borders. But perhaps the most important advantages, such as the carrying on of business between two or more states, are derived through the federal government. Great corporations are protected in a considerable measure from the taxing power and regulatory power of the states by virtue of the interstate character of their businesses. As the profit to such a corporation increases, so the value of its advantages and protection increases.

Furthermore, the drain of a depression upon the reserves of business puts a disproportionate strain upon the modestly capitalized small enterprise. Without such small enterprises our competitive economic society would cease. Size begets monopoly. Moreover, in the aggregate these little businesses furnish the indispensable local basis for those nationwide markets which alone can ensure the success of our mass production industries. Today our smaller corporations are fighting not only for their own local well-being but for that fairly distributed national prosperity which makes large-scale enterprise possible.

It seems only equitable, therefore, to adjust our tax system in accordance with economic capacity, advantage and fact. The smaller corporations should not carry burdens beyond their powers; the vast concentrations of capital should be ready to carry burdens commensurate with their powers and their advantages.

We have established the principle of graduated taxation in respect to personal incomes, gifts, and estates. We should apply the same principle to corporations. Today the smallest corporation pays the same rate on its net profits as the corporation which is a thousand times its size.

I, therefore, recommend the substitution of a corporation income tax graduated according to the size of corporation income in place of the present uniform corporation income tax . . .

18.

This Measure Gives at Least Some Protection to Thirty Millions of Our Citizens

Statement on Signing the Social Security Act
August 14, 1935

In signing the Social Security Act, Roosevelt was not only moving the United States—the nation which had led the way in making public education a universal right—all the more in the direction of social democracy, but also acting to make the self-evident truth that all men (and women) had a right to life, liberty, and the pursuit of happiness all the more real. Sadly, as significant as the Act was, the law and the program were not as comprehensive as FDR himself had hoped they would be. Conservatives in and out of Congress succeeded in blocking the inclusion of national health care in it. And white supremacist Southern Democrats blocked vast numbers of African Americans from enjoying the benefits of the new program by excluding agricultural workers and household workers from its provisions.

Today a hope of many years' standing is in large part fulfilled. The civilization of the past hundred years, with its startling industrial changes, has tended more and more to make life insecure. Young people have come to wonder what would be their lot when they came to old age. The man with a job has wondered how long the job would last.

This social security measure gives at least some protection to thirty millions of our citizens who will reap direct benefits through unemployment compensation, through old-age pensions, and through increased services for the protection of children and the prevention of ill health.

We can never insure one hundred percent of the population against one hundred percent of the hazards and vicissitudes of life, but we have tried to frame a law which will give some measure of protection to the average citizen and to his family against the loss of a job and against poverty-ridden old age.

This law, too, represents a cornerstone in a structure which is being built but is by no means complete. It is a structure intended to lessen the force of possible future depressions. It will act as a protection to future administrations against the necessity of going deeply into debt to furnish relief to the needy. The law will flatten out the peaks and valleys of deflation and of inflation. It is, in short, a law that will take care of human needs and at the same time provide for the United States an economic structure of vastly greater soundness . . .

19.

Popular Opinion Is at War with a Power-Seeking Minority

Annual Message to Congress
Washington, DC, January 3, 1936

In his 1936 Annual Message to Congress, Roosevelt came out strongly against both the rise of autocracy overseas and the rising threat of renewed autocracy in the United States. Everyone knew he was referring on the one hand to the spread of Fascism in Europe and, on the other, to the efforts at home by many of the most powerful and wealthiest corporate figures in America, organized in a group called the Liberty League, to not simply persuade Americans—through well-funded propaganda campaigns—that the New Deal was "un-American," but also bring an end to FDR's presidency at the upcoming elections in November.

Mr. President, Mr. Speaker, Members of the Senate and of the House of Representatives:

We are about to enter upon another year of the responsibility which the electorate of the United States has placed in our hands. Having come so far, it is fitting that we should pause to survey the ground which we have covered and the path which lies ahead.

On the fourth day of March, 1933, on the occasion of taking the oath of office as president of the United States, I addressed the people of our country. Need I recall either the scene or the national circumstances attending the occasion? The crisis of that moment was almost exclusively a national one. In recognition of that fact, so obvious to the millions in the streets and in the homes of America, I devoted by far the greater part of that address to what I called, and the nation called, critical days within our own borders.

You will remember that on that fourth of March, 1933, the world picture was an image of substantial peace. International consultation and widespread hope for the bettering of relations between the nations gave to all of us a reasonable expectation that the barriers to mutual confidence, to increased trade, and to the peaceful settlement of disputes could be progressively removed. In fact, my only reference to the field of world policy in that address was in these words: "I would dedicate this nation to the policy of the good neighbor—the neighbor who resolutely respects himself and, because he does so, respects the rights of others—a neighbor who respects his obligations and respects the sanctity of his agreements in and with a world of neighbors."

In the years that have followed, that sentiment has remained the dedication of this nation. . . .

The rest of the world—Ah! there is the rub.

Were I today to deliver an inaugural address to the people of the United States, I could not limit my comments on world affairs to one paragraph. With much regret I should be compelled to devote the greater part to world affairs. Since the summer of that same year of 1933, the temper and the purposes of the rulers of many of the great populations in Europe and in Asia have not pointed the way either to peace or to goodwill among men. . . .

On those other continents many nations, principally the smaller peoples, if left to themselves, would be content with their boundaries and willing to solve within themselves and in cooperation with their neighbors their individual problems, both economic and social. The rulers of those nations, deep in their hearts, follow these peaceful and reasonable aspirations of their peoples. These rulers must remain ever vigilant against the possibility today or tomorrow of invasion or attack by the rulers of other peoples who fail to subscribe to the principles of bettering the human race by peaceful means.

Within those other nations—those which today must bear the primary, definite responsibility for jeopardizing world peace—what hope lies? To say the least, there are grounds for pessimism. It is idle for us or for others to preach that the masses of the people who constitute those nations which are dominated by the twin spirits of autocracy and aggression are out of sympathy with their rulers, that they are allowed no opportunity to express themselves, that they would change things if they could.

That, unfortunately, is not so clear. It might be true that the masses of the people in those nations would change the policies of their governments if they could be allowed full freedom and full access to the processes of democratic government as we understand them. But they do not have that access; lacking it they follow blindly and fervently the lead of those who seek autocratic power. . . .

I recognize and you will recognize that these words which I have chosen with deliberation will not prove popular in any nation that chooses to fit this shoe to its foot. Such sentiments, however, will find sympathy and understanding in those nations where the people themselves are honestly desirous of peace but must constantly align themselves on one side or the other in the kaleidoscopic jockeying for position which is characteristic of European and Asiatic relations today. For the peace-loving nations, and there are many of them, find that their very identity depends on their moving and moving again on the chess board of international politics.

I suggested in the spring of 1933 that 85 or 90 percent of all the people in the world were content with the territorial limits of their respective nations and were willing further to reduce their armed forces if every other nation in the world would agree to do likewise.

That is equally true today, and it is even more true today that world peace and world goodwill are blocked by only 10 or 15 percent of the world's population. That is why efforts to reduce armies have thus far not only failed, but have been met by vastly increased armaments on land and in the air. That is why even efforts to continue the existing limits on naval armaments into the years to come show such little current success.

But the policy of the United States has been clear and consistent. We have sought with earnestness in every possible way to limit world armaments and to attain the peaceful solution of disputes among all nations.

We have sought by every legitimate means to exert our moral influence against repression, against intolerance, against autocracy, and in favor of freedom of expression, equality before the law, religious tolerance, and popular rule.

In the field of commerce we have undertaken to encourage a more reasonable interchange of the world's goods. In the field of international finance we have, so far as we are concerned, put an end to dollar diplomacy, to money grabbing, to speculation for the benefit of the powerful and the rich, at the expense of the small and the poor.

As a consistent part of a clear policy, the United States is following a twofold neutrality toward any and all nations which engage in wars that are not of immediate concern to the Americas. First, we decline to encourage the prosecution of war by permitting belligerents to obtain arms, ammunition, or implements of war from the United States. Second, we seek to discourage the use by belligerent nations of any and all American products calculated to facilitate the prosecution of a war in quantities over and above our normal exports of them in time of peace.

I trust that these objectives thus clearly and unequivocally stated will be carried forward by cooperation between this Congress and the president.

I realize that I have emphasized to you the gravity of the situation which confronts the people of the world. This emphasis is justified because of its importance to civilization and therefore to the United States. Peace is jeopardized by the few and not by the many. Peace is threatened by those who seek selfish power. The world has witnessed similar eras—as in the days when petty kings and feudal barons were changing the map of Europe every fortnight, or when great emperors and great kings were engaged in a mad scramble for colonial empire.

We hope that we are not again at the threshold of such an era. But if face it we must, then the United States and the rest of the Americas can play but one role: through a well-ordered neutrality . . .

The evidence before us clearly proves that autocracy in world affairs endangers peace and that such threats do not spring from those nations devoted to the democratic ideal. If this be true in world affairs, it should have the greatest weight in the determination of domestic policies.

Within democratic nations the chief concern of the people is to prevent the continuance or the rise of autocratic institutions that beget slavery at home and aggression abroad. Within our borders, as in the world at large, popular opinion is at war with a power-seeking minority.

That is no new thing. It was fought out in the Constitutional Convention of 1787. From time to time since then, the battle has been continued, under Thomas Jefferson, Andrew Jackson, Theodore Roosevelt, and Woodrow Wilson.

In these latter years we have witnessed the domination of government by financial and industrial groups, numerically small but politically dominant in the twelve years that succeeded the World War. The present group of which I speak is indeed numerically small and, while it exercises a large influence and has much to say in the world of business, it does not, I am confident, speak the true sentiments of the less articulate but more important elements that constitute real American business.

In March 1933, I appealed to the Congress of the United States and to the people of the United States in a new effort to restore power to those to whom it rightfully belonged. The response to that appeal resulted in the writing of a new chapter in the history of popular government. You, the members of the legislative branch, and I, the executive, contended for and established a new relationship between government and people.

What were the terms of that new relationship? They were an appeal from the clamor of many private and selfish interests, yes, an appeal from the clamor of partisan interest, to the ideal of the public interest. Government became the representative and the trustee of the public interest. Our aim was to build upon essentially democratic institutions, seeking all the while the adjustment of burdens, the help of the needy, the protection of the weak, the liberation of the exploited and the genuine protection of the people's property.

It goes without saying that to create such an economic constitutional order, more than a single legislative enactment was called for. We, you in the Congress and I as the executive, had to build upon a broad base. Now, after thirty-four months of work, we contemplate a fairly rounded whole. We have returned the control of the federal government to the city of Washington.

To be sure, in so doing, we have invited battle. We have earned the hatred of entrenched greed. The very nature of the problem that we faced made it necessary to drive some people from power and strictly to regulate others. I made that plain when I took the oath of office in March 1933. I spoke of the practices of the unscrupulous money-changers who stood indicted in the court of public opinion. I spoke of the rulers of the exchanges of mankind's goods, who failed through their own stubbornness and their own incompetence. I said that they had admitted their failure and had abdicated.

Abdicated? Yes, in 1933, but now with the passing of danger they forget their damaging admissions and withdraw their abdication.

They seek the restoration of their selfish power. They offer to lead us back round the same old corner into the same old dreary street.

Yes, there are still determined groups that are intent upon that very thing. Rigorously held up to popular examination, their true character presents itself. They steal the livery of great national constitutional ideals to serve discredited special interests. As guardians and trustees for great groups of individual stockholders they wrongfully seek to carry the property and the interests entrusted to them into the arena of partisan politics. They seek—this minority in business and industry—to control and often do control and use for their own purposes legitimate and highly honored business associations; they engage in vast propaganda to spread fear and discord among the people—they would "gang up" against the people's liberties.

The principle that they would instill into government if they succeed in seizing power is well shown by the principles which many of them have instilled into their own affairs: autocracy toward labor, toward stockholders, toward consumers, toward public sentiment. Autocrats in smaller things, they seek autocracy in bigger things. "By their fruits ye shall know them."

If these gentlemen believe, as they say they believe, that the measures adopted by this Congress and its predecessor, and carried out by this administration, have hindered rather than promoted recovery, let them be consistent. Let them propose to this Congress the complete repeal of these measures. The way is open to such a proposal.

Let action be positive and not negative. The way is open in the Congress of the United States for an expression of opinion by yeas and nays. Shall we say that values are restored and that the Congress will, therefore, repeal the laws under which we have been bringing them back? Shall we say that because national income has grown with rising prosperity, we shall repeal existing taxes and thereby put off the day of approaching a balanced budget and of starting to reduce the national debt? Shall we abandon the reasonable support and regulation of banking? Shall we restore the dollar to its former gold content?

Shall we say to the farmer, "The prices for your products are in part restored. Now go and hoe your own row"?

Shall we say to the home owners, "We have reduced your rates of interest. We have no further concern with how you keep your home or what you pay for your money. That is your affair"?

Shall we say to the several millions of unemployed citizens who face the very problem of existence, of getting enough to eat, "We will withdraw from giving you work. We will turn you back to the charity of your communities and those men of selfish power who tell you that perhaps they will employ you if the government leaves them strictly alone"?

Shall we say to the needy unemployed, "Your problem is a local one except that perhaps the federal government, as an act of mere generosity, will be willing to pay to your city or to your county a few grudging dollars to help maintain your soup kitchens"?

Shall we say to the children who have worked all day in the factories, "Child labor is a local issue and so are your starvation wages; something to be solved or left unsolved by the jurisdiction of forty-eight states"?

Shall we say to the laborer, "Your right to organize, your relations with your employer have nothing to do with the public interest; if your employer will not even meet with you to discuss your problems and his, that is none of our affair"?

Shall we say to the unemployed and the aged, "Social security lies not within the province of the federal government; you must seek relief elsewhere"?

Shall we say to the men and women who live in conditions of squalor in country and in city, "The health and the happiness of you and your children are no concern of ours"?

Shall we expose our population once more by the repeal of laws which protect them against the loss of their honest investments and against the manipulations of dishonest speculators? Shall we abandon the splendid efforts of the federal government to raise the health standards of the nation and to give youth a decent opportunity through such means as the Civilian Conservation Corps?

Members of the Congress, let these challenges be met. If this is what these gentlemen want, let them say so to the Congress of the United States. Let them no longer hide their dissent in a cowardly cloak of generality. Let them define the issue. We have been specific in our affirmative action. Let them be specific in their negative attack.

But the challenge faced by this Congress is more menacing than merely a return to the past—bad as that would be. Our resplendent economic autocracy does not want to return to that individualism of which they prate, even though the advantages under that system went to the ruthless and the strong. They realize that in thirty-four months we have built up new instruments of public power. In the hands of a people's government this power is wholesome and proper. But in the hands of political puppets of an economic autocracy such power would provide shackles for the liberties of the people. Give them their way and they will take the course of every autocracy of the past—power for themselves, enslavement for the public.

Their weapon is the weapon of fear. I have said, "The only thing we have to fear is fear itself." That is as true today as it was in 1933. But such fear as they instill today is not a natural fear, a normal fear; it is a synthetic, manufactured, poisonous fear that is being spread subtly, expensively, and cleverly by the same people who cried in those other days, "Save us, save us, lest we perish."

I am confident that the Congress of the United States well understands the facts and is ready to wage unceasing warfare against those who seek a continuation of that spirit of fear. The carrying out of the laws of the land as enacted by the Congress requires protection until final adjudication by the highest tribunal of the land. The Congress has the right and can find the means to protect its own prerogatives.

We are justified in our present confidence. . . .

In the light of our substantial material progress, in the light of the increasing effectiveness of the restoration of popular rule, I recommend to the Congress that we advance; that we do not retreat. I have confidence that you will not fail the people of the nation whose mandate you have already so faithfully fulfilled. . . .

20.

This Generation Has a Rendezvous with Destiny

Re-nomination Acceptance Speech at Democratic National Convention
Philadelphia, Pennsylvania, June 27, 1936

Accepting the Democratic nomination for a second term as president at the party's national convention, Roosevelt delivered the most radical speech ever given by a serving president. He compared the struggles of the day to those of the American Revolution. Just as Americans fought to free themselves from political royalism, autocracy, and tyranny in the 1770s, he boldly stated, Americans of the 1930s were now fighting to free themselves from economic royalism, autocracy, and tyranny. Indeed, he declared: "These economic royalists complain that we seek to overthrow the institutions of America. What they really complain of is that we seek to take away their power. Our allegiance to American institutions requires the overthrow of this kind of power."

Senator Robinson, members of the Democratic Convention, my friends:

Here, and in every community throughout the land, we are met at a time of great moment to the future of the nation. It is an occasion to be dedicated to the simple and sincere expression of an attitude toward problems, the determination of which will profoundly affect America.

I come not only as a leader of a party, not only as a candidate for high office, but as one upon whom many critical hours have imposed and still impose a grave responsibility.

For the sympathy, help and confidence with which Americans have sustained me in my task I am grateful. . . .

America will not forget these recent years, will not forget that the rescue was not a mere party task. It was the concern of all of us. In our strength we rose together, rallied our energies together, applied the old rules of common sense, and together survived.

In those days we feared fear. That was why we fought fear. And today, my friends, we have won against the most dangerous of our foes. We have conquered fear.

But I cannot, with candor, tell you that all is well with the world. Clouds of suspicion, tides of ill-will and intolerance gather darkly in many places. In our own land we enjoy indeed a fullness of life greater than that of most nations. But the rush of modern civilization itself has raised for us new difficulties, new problems which must be solved if we are to preserve to the United States the political and economic freedom for which Washington and Jefferson planned and fought.

Philadelphia is a good city in which to write American history. This is fitting ground on which to reaffirm the faith of our fathers; to pledge ourselves to restore to the people a wider freedom; to give to 1936 as the founders gave to 1776—an American way of life.

That very word freedom, in itself and of necessity, suggests freedom from some restraining power. In 1776 we sought freedom from the tyranny of a political autocracy—from the eighteenth-century royalists who held special privileges from the crown. It was to perpetuate their privilege that they governed without the consent of the governed; that they denied the right of free assembly and free speech; that they restricted the worship of God; that they put the average man's property and the average man's life in pawn to the mercenaries of dynastic power; that they regimented the people.

And so it was to win freedom from the tyranny of political autocracy that the American Revolution was fought. That victory gave the business of governing into the hands of the average man, who won the right with his neighbors to make and order his own destiny through his own government. Political tyranny was wiped out at Philadelphia on July 4, 1776.

Since that struggle, however, man's inventive genius released new forces in our land which reordered the lives of our people . . . The age of machinery, of railroads; of steam and electricity; the telegraph and the radio; mass production, mass distribution—all of these combined to bring forward a new civilization and with it a new problem for those who sought to remain free.

For out of this modern civilization economic royalists carved new dynasties. New kingdoms were built upon concentration of control over material things. Through new uses of corporations, banks and securities, new machinery of industry and agriculture, of labor and capital—all undreamed of by the fathers—the whole structure of modern life was impressed into this royal service.

There was no place among this royalty for our many thousands of small business men and merchants who sought to make a worthy use of the American system of initiative and profit. They were no more free than the worker or the farmer. Even honest and progressive-minded men of wealth, aware of their obligation to their generation, could never know just where they fitted into this dynastic scheme of things.

It was natural and perhaps human that the privileged princes of these new economic dynasties, thirsting for power, reached out for control over government itself. They created a new despotism and wrapped it in the robes of legal sanction. In its service new mercenaries sought to regiment the people, their labor, and their property. And as a result the average man once more confronts the problem that faced the Minute Man.

The hours men and women worked, the wages they received, the conditions of their labor—these had passed beyond the control of the people, and were imposed by this new industrial dictatorship. The savings of the average family, the capital of the small business man, the investments set aside for old age—other people's money—these were tools which the new economic royalty used to dig itself in.

Those who tilled the soil no longer reaped the rewards which were their right. The small measure of their gains was decreed by men in distant cities.

Throughout the nation, opportunity was limited by monopoly. Individual initiative was crushed in the cogs of a great machine. The field open for free business was more and more restricted. Private enterprise, indeed, became too private. It became privileged enterprise, not free enterprise.

An old English judge once said: "Necessitous men are not free men." Liberty requires opportunity to make a living—a living decent according to the standard of the time, a living which gives man not only enough to live by, but something to live for.

For too many of us the political equality we once had won was meaningless in the face of economic inequality. A small group had concentrated into their own hands an almost complete control over other people's property, other people's money, other people's labor—other people's lives. For too many of us life was no longer free; liberty no longer real; men could no longer follow the pursuit of happiness.

Against economic tyranny such as this, the American citizen could appeal only to the organized power of government. The collapse of 1929 showed up the despotism for what it was. The election of 1932 was the people's mandate to end it. Under that mandate it is being ended.

The royalists of the economic order have conceded that political freedom was the business of the government, but they have maintained that economic slavery was nobody's business. They granted that the government could protect the citizen in his right to vote, but they denied that the government could do anything to protect the citizen in his right to work and his right to live.

Today we stand committed to the proposition that freedom is no half-and-half affair. If the average citizen is guaranteed equal opportunity in the polling place, he must have equal opportunity in the market place.

These economic royalists complain that we seek to overthrow the institutions of America. What they really complain of is that we seek to take away their power. Our allegiance to American institutions requires the overthrow of this kind of power. In vain they seek to hide behind the Flag and the Constitution. In their blindness they forget what the Flag and the Constitution stand for. Now, as always, they stand for democracy, not tyranny; for freedom, not subjection; and against a dictatorship by mob rule and the over-privileged alike.

The brave and clear platform adopted by this convention, to which I heartily subscribe, sets forth that government in a modern civilization has certain inescapable obligations to its citizens, among which are protection of the family and the home, the establishment of a democracy of opportunity, and aid to those overtaken by disaster.

But the resolute enemy within our gates is ever ready to beat down our words unless in greater courage we will fight for them.

For more than three years we have fought for them. This convention, in every word and deed, has pledged that that fight will go on.

The defeats and victories of these years have given to us as a people a new understanding of our government and of ourselves. Never since the early days of the New England town meeting have the affairs of government been so widely discussed and so clearly appreciated. It has been brought home to us that the only effective guide for the safety of this most worldly of worlds, the greatest guide of all, is moral principle.

We do not see faith, hope, and charity as unattainable ideals, but we use them as stout supports of a nation fighting the fight for freedom in a modern civilization.

Faith—in the soundness of democracy in the midst of dictatorships.

Hope—renewed because we know so well the progress we have made.

Charity—in the true spirit of that grand old word. For charity literally translated from the original means love, the love that understands, that does not merely share the wealth of the giver, but in true sympathy and wisdom helps men to help themselves.

We seek not merely to make government a mechanical implement, but to give it the vibrant personal character that is the very embodiment of human charity.

We are poor indeed if this nation cannot afford to lift from every recess of American life the dread fear of the unemployed that they are not needed in the world. We cannot afford to accumulate a deficit in the books of human fortitude.

In the place of the palace of privilege we seek to build a temple out of faith and hope and charity.

It is a sobering thing, my friends, to be a servant of this great cause. We try in our daily work to remember that the cause belongs not to us, but to the people. The standard is not in the hands of you and me alone. It is carried by America. We seek daily to profit from experience, to learn to do better as our task proceeds.

Governments can err, presidents do make mistakes, but the immortal Dante tells us that divine justice weighs the sins of the cold-blooded and the sins of the warm-hearted in different scales.

Better the occasional faults of a government that lives in a spirit of charity than the consistent omissions of a government frozen in the ice of its own indifference.

There is a mysterious cycle in human events. To some generations much is given. Of other generations much is expected. This generation of Americans has a rendezvous with destiny.

In this world of ours in other lands, there are some people, who, in times past, have lived and fought for freedom, and seem to have grown too weary to carry on the fight. They have sold their heritage of freedom for the illusion of a living. They have yielded their democracy.

I believe in my heart that only our success can stir their ancient hope. They begin to know that here in America we are waging a great and successful war. It is not alone a war against want and destitution and economic demoralization. It is more than that; it is a war for the survival of democracy. We are fighting to save a great and precious form of government for ourselves and for the world.

I accept the commission you have tendered me. I join with you. I am enlisted for the duration of the war.

21.

A True Patriotism Urges Us to Build an Even More Substantial America . . .

Speech Dedicating a World War Memorial
St. Louis, Missouri, October 14, 1936

Speaking at the dedication of a World War I war memorial, FDR not only honored those who had fought and died, but also spoke of another kind of service and patriotism, no less essential to the future of a democratic nation.

You and I join here with the rest of the nation in dedicating this site as a memorial to the valiant dead of the World War. Here will rise a fitting structure—a symbol of devoted patriotism and unselfish service.

We in America do not build monuments to war. We do not build monuments to conquest. We build monuments to commemorate the spirit of sacrifice in war—reminders of our desire for peace.

The memory of those whom the War called to the beyond urges us to consecrate the best that is in us to the service of country in times of peace. We best honor the memory of those dead by striving for peace, that the terror of the days of war will be with us no more. In what we have done during the last three years to promote national recovery at home, to extend the hand of the good neighbor to the nations of the world, to break down the barriers to commerce which divide nation from nation, we are promoting the course of peace throughout the world.

Here at home is the call to service too.

Inequalities in our social order call for correction. A true patriotism urges us to build an even more substantial America where the good things of life may be shared by more of us, where the social injustices will not be encouraged to flourish. The many different occupations in our economic and social order can and must be tied more closely together for their mutual advantage and for the advantage of America.

It is significant that the site of this memorial to the veterans of the World War is also the site of the beginning of the old Oregon trail. Here those pioneers of old left to begin that long trek across an unknown country. They faced the dangers ahead of them with stout heart and determined mind. They carried the civilization of their day to new outposts. They carried the spirit of America to a broader destiny.

We seek to follow their example along another trail. They turned not back. Let us not turn back in what we seek in these years, for our goal is a sounder and more permanent well-being in America.

We honor them and we will carry on.

May the beauty of the monument which is rising on this site cast a beneficent light on the memories of our comrades, may its substantial structure typify the strength of their purpose, and may it inspire future generations with the desire to be of service to their fellows and their country...

No place could be more fitting to reaffirm that faith and confidence than a monument to those who have died in a gallant effort to save democracy for the world. No place could be more fitting to renew our resolve that that faith will guide us and direct these our efforts of today. May we keep the faith.

22.

I See One-Third of a Nation Ill-Housed, Ill-Clad, Ill-Nourished

Second Inaugural Address
Washington, DC, January 20, 1937

FDR won reelection in November 1936 in an historic landslide. In fact, not only did he receive 28 million votes versus 16.7 million for the Republican nominee, Kansas governor Alf Landon, but also the Democrats further increased their control of both houses of Congress. In his second inaugural address, Roosevelt projected what might be called a Third New Deal to not only tackle the persistent economic depression, but also confront the persistent poverty that so many Americans were enduring.

When four years ago we met to inaugurate a president, the Republic, single-minded in anxiety, stood in spirit here. We dedicated ourselves to the fulfillment of a vision—to speed the time when there would be for all the people that security and peace essential to the pursuit of happiness. We of the Republic pledged ourselves to drive from the temple of our ancient faith those who had profaned it; to end by action, tireless and unafraid, the stagnation and despair of that day. We did those first things first.

Our covenant with ourselves did not stop there. Instinctively we recognized a deeper need—the need to find through government the instrument of our united purpose to solve for the individual the ever-rising problems of a complex civilization. . . .

We of the Republic sensed the truth that democratic government has innate capacity to protect its people against disasters once considered inevitable, to solve problems once considered unsolvable. We would not admit that we could not find a way to master economic epidemics just as, after centuries of fatalistic suffering, we had found a way to master epidemics of disease. We refused to leave the problems of our common welfare to be solved by the winds of chance and the hurricanes of disaster.

In this we Americans were discovering no wholly new truth; we were writing a new chapter in our book of self-government.

This year marks the one hundred and fiftieth anniversary of the Constitutional Convention which made us a nation. At that Convention our forefathers found the way out of the chaos which followed the Revolutionary War; they created a strong government with powers of united action sufficient then and now to solve problems utterly beyond individual or local solution. A century and a half ago they established the federal government in order to promote the general welfare and secure the blessings of liberty to the American people.

Today we invoke those same powers of government to achieve the same objectives.

Four years of new experience have not belied our historic instinct. They hold out the clear hope that government within communities, government within the separate states, and government of the United States can do the things the times require, without yielding its democracy. Our tasks in the last four years did not force democracy to take a holiday.

Nearly all of us recognize that as intricacies of human relationships increase, so power to govern them also must increase power to stop evil; power to do good. The essential democracy of our nation and the safety of our people depend not upon the absence of power, but upon lodging it with those whom the people can change or continue at stated intervals through an honest and free system of elections. The Constitution of 1787 did not make our democracy impotent.

In fact, in these last four years, we have made the exercise of all power more democratic; for we have begun to bring private autocratic powers into their proper subordination to the public's government. The legend that they were invincible above and beyond the processes of a democracy—has been shattered. They have been challenged and beaten.

Our progress out of the Depression is obvious. But that is not all that you and I mean by the new order of things. Our pledge was not merely to do a patchwork job with secondhand materials. By using the new materials of social justice we have undertaken to erect on the old foundations a more enduring structure for the better use of future generations. . . .

This new understanding undermines the old admiration of worldly success as such. We are beginning to abandon our tolerance of the abuse of power by those who betray for profit the elementary decencies of life.

In this process evil things formerly accepted will not be so easily con-doned. Hardheadedness will not so easily excuse hardheartedness. We are moving toward an era of good feeling. But we realize that there can be no era of good feeling save among men of good will.

For these reasons I am justified in believing that the greatest change we have witnessed has been the change in the moral climate of America.

Among men of good will, science and democracy together offer an ever-richer life and ever-larger satisfaction to the individual. With this change in our moral climate and our rediscovered ability to improve our economic order, we have set our feet upon the road of enduring progress.

Shall we pause now and turn our back upon the road that lies ahead? Shall we call this the promised land? Or, shall we continue on our way? For "each age is a dream that is dying, or one that is coming to birth. . . ."

Let us ask again: Have we reached the goal of our vision of that fourth day of March, 1933? Have we found our happy valley?

I see a great nation, upon a great continent, blessed with a great wealth of natural resources. Its hundred and thirty million people are at peace among themselves; they are making their country a good neighbor among the nations. I see a United States which can demonstrate that, under dem-ocratic methods of government, national wealth can be translated into a spreading volume of human comforts hitherto unknown, and the lowest standard of living can be raised far above the level of mere subsistence.

But here is the challenge to our democracy: In this nation I see tens of millions of its citizens—a substantial part of its whole population—who at this very moment are denied the greater part of what the very lowest standards of today call the necessities of life.

I see millions of families trying to live on incomes so meager that the pall of family disaster hangs over them day by day.

I see millions whose daily lives in city and on farm continue under conditions labeled indecent by a so-called polite society half a century ago.

I see millions denied education, recreation, and the opportunity to bet-ter their lot and the lot of their children.

I see millions lacking the means to buy the products of farm and factory and by their poverty denying work and productiveness to many other millions.

I see one-third of a nation ill-housed, ill-clad, ill-nourished.

It is not in despair that I paint you that picture. I paint it for you in hope—because the nation, seeing and understanding the injustice in it, proposes to paint it out. We are determined to make every American citizen the subject of his country's interest and concern; and we will never regard any faithful, law-abiding group within our borders as superfluous. The test of our progress is not whether we add more to the abundance of those who have much; it is whether we provide enough for those who have too little. . . .

Overwhelmingly, we of the Republic are men and women of good will; men and women who have more than warm hearts of dedication; men and women who have cool heads and willing hands of practical purpose as well. They will insist that every agency of popular government use effective instruments to carry out their will.

Government is competent when all who compose it work as trustees for the whole people. It can make constant progress when it keeps abreast of all the facts. It can obtain justified support and legitimate criticism when the people receive true information of all that government does.

If I know aught of the will of our people, they will demand that these conditions of effective government shall be created and maintained. They will demand a nation uncorrupted by cancers of injustice and, therefore, strong among the nations in its example of the will to peace.

Today we reconsecrate our country to long-cherished ideals in a suddenly changed civilization. In every land there are always at work forces that drive men apart and forces that draw men together. In our personal ambitions we are individualists. But in our seeking for economic and political progress as a nation, we all go up, or else we all go down, as one people.

To maintain a democracy of effort requires a vast amount of patience in dealing with differing methods, a vast amount of humility. But out of the confusion of many voices rises an understanding of dominant public need. Then political leadership can voice common ideals, and aid in their realization.

In taking again the oath of office as president of the United States, I assume the solemn obligation of leading the American people forward along the road over which they have chosen to advance.

While this duty rests upon me I shall do my utmost to speak their purpose and to do their will, seeking Divine guidance to help us each and every one to give light to them that sit in darkness and to guide our feet into the way of peace.

23.

The Constitution Is a Layman's Document, Not a Lawyer's Contract

Address on Constitution Day
Washington, DC, September 17, 1937

In 1936, the still conservative-dominated Supreme Court had declared key elements of the New Deal's National Industrial Recovery Act (1933) and Agricultural Adjustment Act (1933) unconstitutional. The decisions led Roosevelt to propose expanding the number of seats on the Court in order to place more liberal justices on it—he feared that if he did not, the conservatives on the Court would find both the new Social Security Act and the National Labor Relations Act (NLRA) unconstitutional as well. In this address, delivered on Constitution Day, FDR offered arguments to bolster his projected plan. Nonetheless, significant opposition arose from both Republicans and Democrats, which led him to retreat. Yet to the surprise of many, not only did the Court find both Social Security and the NLRA constitutional in 1937, but the president would also soon get to both appoint seven new justices and name a new Chief Justice. All of which initiated what some scholars have called a "constitutional revolution" as the Court gave increasing priority to "human rights" over "property rights."

My fellow Americans:

One hundred fifty years ago tonight, thirty-eight weary delegates to a Convention in Philadelphia signed the Constitution. Four handwritten sheets of parchment were enough to state the terms on which thirteen independent weak little republics agreed to try to survive together as one strong nation.

A third of the original delegates had given up and gone home. The moral force of Washington and Franklin had kept the rest together. Those remained who cared the most; and caring most, dared most.

The world of 1787 provided a perfect opportunity for the organization of a new form of government thousands of miles removed from influences hostile to it. How we then governed ourselves did not greatly concern Europe. And what occurred in Europe did not immediately affect us.

Today the picture is different.

Now what we do has enormous immediate effect not only among the nations of Europe but also among those of the Americas and the Far East, and what in any part of the world they do as surely and quickly affects us.

In such an atmosphere our generation has watched democracies replace monarchies which had failed their people, and dictatorships displace democracies which had failed to function. And of late we have heard a clear challenge to the democratic idea of representative government. . . .

The people of America are rightly determined to keep that growing menace from our shores.

The known and measurable danger of becoming involved in war we face confidently. As to that, your government knows your mind, and you know your government's mind.

But it takes even more foresight, intelligence, and patience to meet the subtle attack which spreading dictatorship makes upon the morale of a democracy.

In our generation, a new idea has come to dominate thought about government, the idea that the resources of the nation can be made to produce a far higher standard of living for the masses of the people if only government is intelligent and energetic in giving the right direction to economic life.

That idea—or more properly that ideal—is wholly justified by the facts. It cannot be thrust aside by those who want to go back to the conditions of ten years ago or even preserve the conditions of today. It puts all forms of government to their proof.

That ideal makes understandable the demands of labor for shorter hours and higher wages, the demands of farmers for a more stable income, the demands of the great majority of business men for relief from disruptive trade practices, the demands of all for the end of that kind of license, often mistermed "Liberty," which permits a handful of the population to take far more than its tolerable share from the rest of the people.

And as other forms of government in other lands parade their pseudo-science of economic organization, even some of our own people may wonder whether democracy can match dictatorship in giving this generation the things it wants from government.

We have those who really fear the majority rule of democracy, who want old forms of economic and social control to remain in a few hands. They say in their hearts: "If constitutional democracy continues to threaten our control why should we be against a plutocratic dictatorship if that would perpetuate our control?"

And we have those who are in too much of a hurry, who are impatient at the processes of constitutional democracies, who want Utopia overnight and are not sure that some vague form of proletarian dictatorship is not the quickest road to it.

Both types are equally dangerous. One represents cold-blooded resolve to hold power. We have engaged in a definite, and so far successful, contest against that. The other represents a reckless resolve to seize power. Equally we are against that.

And the overwhelming majority of the American people fully understand and completely approve that course as the course of the present government of the United States.

To hold to that course our constitutional democratic form of government must meet the insistence of the great mass of our people that economic and social security and the standard of American living be raised from what they are to levels which the people know our resources justify.

Only by succeeding in that can we ensure against internal doubt as to the worthwhileness of our democracy and dissipate the illusion that the necessary price of efficiency is dictatorship with its attendant spirit of aggression.

That is why I have been saying for months that there is a crisis in American affairs which demands action now, a crisis particularly dangerous because its external and internal difficulties re-enforce each other.

Purposely I paint a broad picture. For only if the problem is seen in perspective can we see its solution in perspective.

I am not a pessimist. I believe that democratic government in this country can do all the things which commonsense people, seeing that picture as a whole, have the right to expect. I believe that these things can be done under the Constitution, without the surrender of a single one of the civil and religious liberties it was intended to safeguard.

And I am determined that under the Constitution these things shall be done.

The men who wrote the Constitution were the men who fought the Revolution. They had watched a weak emergency government almost lose the war, and continue economic distress among thirteen little republics, at peace but without effective national government.

So when these men planned a new government, they drew the kind of agreement which men make when they really want to work together under it for a very long time.

For the youngest of nations they drew what is today the oldest written instrument under which men have continuously lived together as a nation.

The Constitution of the United States was a layman's document, not a lawyer's contract. That cannot be stressed too often. Madison, most responsible for it, was not a lawyer; nor was Washington or Franklin, whose sense of the give-and-take of life had kept the Convention together.

This great layman's document was a charter of general principles, completely different from the "whereases" and the "parties of the first part" and the fine print which lawyers put into leases and insurance policies and installment agreements.

When the Framers were dealing with what they rightly considered eternal verities, unchangeable by time and circumstance, they used specific language. In no uncertain terms, for instance, they forbade titles of nobility, the suspension of habeas corpus, and the withdrawal of money from the Treasury except after appropriation by law. With almost equal definiteness they detailed the Bill of Rights.

But when they considered the fundamental powers of the new national government they used generality, implication, and statement of mere objectives, as intentional phrases which flexible statesmanship of the future, within the Constitution, could adapt to time and circumstance. For instance, the framers used broad and general language capable of meeting evolution and change when they referred to commerce between the states, the taxing power, and the general welfare.

Even the Supreme Court was treated with that purposeful lack of specification. Contrary to the belief of many Americans, the Constitution says nothing about any power of the Court to declare legislation unconstitutional; nor does it mention the number of judges for the Court. Again and again the Convention voted down proposals to give Justices of the Court a veto over legislation. Clearly a majority of the delegates believed that the relation of the Court to the Congress and the executive, like the other subjects treated in general terms, would work itself out by evolution and change over the years.

But for one hundred and fifty years we have had an unending struggle between those who would preserve this original broad concept of the Constitution as a layman's instrument of government and those who would shrivel the Constitution into a lawyer's contract.

Those of us who really believe in the enduring wisdom of the Constitution hold no rancor against those who professionally or politically talk and think in purely legalistic phrases. We cannot seriously be alarmed when they cry "unconstitutional" at every effort to better the condition of our people.

Such cries have always been with us; and, ultimately, they have always been overruled. . . .

That lay rank and file can take cheer from the historic fact that every effort to construe the Constitution as a lawyer's contract rather than a layman's charter has ultimately failed. Whenever legalistic interpretation has clashed with contemporary sense on great questions of broad national policy, ultimately the people and the Congress have had their way.

But that word "ultimately" covers a terrible cost.

It cost a Civil War to gain recognition of the constitutional power of the Congress to legislate for the territories.

It cost twenty years of taxation on those least able to pay to recognize the constitutional power of the Congress to levy taxes on those most able to pay.

It cost twenty years of exploitation of women's labor to recognize the constitutional power of the states to pass minimum wage laws for their protection.

It has cost twenty years already—and no one knows how many more are to come—to obtain a constitutional interpretation that will let the nation regulate the shipment in national commerce of goods sweated from the labor of little children.

We know it takes time to adjust government to the needs of society. But modern history proves that reforms too long delayed or denied have jeopardized peace, undermined democracy and swept away civil and religious liberties.

Yes, time more than ever before is vital in statesmanship and in government, in all three branches of it.

We will no longer be permitted to sacrifice each generation in turn while the law catches up with life.

We can no longer afford the luxury of twenty-year lags.

You will find no justification in any of the language of the Constitution for delay in the reforms which the mass of the American people now demand.

Yet nearly every attempt to meet those demands for social and economic betterment has been jeopardized or actually forbidden by those who have sought to read into the Constitution language which the framers refused to write into the Constitution.

No one cherishes more deeply than I the civil and religious liberties achieved by so much blood and anguish through the many centuries of Anglo-American history. But the Constitution guarantees liberty, not license masquerading as liberty.

Let me put the real situation in the simplest terms. The present government of the United States has never taken away and never will take away any liberty from any minority, unless it be a minority which so abuses its liberty as to do positive and definite harm to its neighbors constituting the majority. But the government of the United States refuses to forget that the Bill of Rights was put into the Constitution not only to protect minorities against intolerance of majorities, but to protect majorities against the enthronement of minorities.

Nothing would so surely destroy the substance of what the Bill of Rights protects than its perversion to prevent social progress. The surest protection of the individual and of minorities is that fundamental tolerance and feeling for fair play which the Bill of Rights assumes. But tolerance and fair play would disappear here as it has in some other lands if the great mass of people were denied confidence in their justice, their security and their self-respect. Desperate people in other lands surrendered their liberties when freedom came merely to mean humiliation and starvation. The crisis of 1933 should make us understand that.

On this solemn anniversary I ask that the American people rejoice in the wisdom of their Constitution.

I ask that they guarantee the effectiveness of each of its parts by living by the Constitution as a whole.

I ask that they have faith in its ultimate capacity to work out the problems of democracy, but that they justify that faith by making it work now rather than twenty years from now.

I ask that they give their fealty to the Constitution itself and not to its misinterpreters.

I ask that they exalt the glorious simplicity of its purposes, rather than a century of complicated legalism.

I ask that majorities and minorities subordinate intolerance and power alike to the common good of all.

For us the Constitution is a common bond, without bitterness, for those who see America as Lincoln saw it, "the last, best hope of earth."

So we revere it, not because it is old but because it is ever new, not in the worship of its past alone but in the faith of the living who keep it young, now and in the years to come.

24.

There Is Little Difference Between the Feudal System and the Fascist System

Address at Gainesville
Gainesville, Georgia, March 23, 1938

Though the New Deal was bringing significant change to the South, the region was still marked by one-party (Democratic) political rule; white supremacy and racial segregation; fierce opposition to labor unions by business; voter suppression by way of poll taxes, literacy tests, and outright violence; and high rates of poverty among whites and blacks alike. In this speech, FDR—who was beloved by both urban and rural working people—spoke his mind about the state of the South. Hoping to shake things up and encourage democratic change, he said: "When you come down to it, there is little difference between the feudal system and the Fascist system. If you believe in the one, you lean to the other."

This celebration, the outward and visible commemoration of the rebirth of Gainesville, is more than a symbol of the fine courage which has made it possible for this city to come back after it had been, in great part, destroyed by the tornado of 1936. These ceremonies touch the interest and life of the whole nation because they typify citizenship which is latent in the American character but which too often remains quiescent and too seldom expresses itself. You were not content to clear away the debris which I, myself, saw as I passed through Gainesville a couple of days after the disaster. You were not content with rebuilding along the lines of the old community. You were not content with throwing yourselves on the help which could be given to you by your state and by the federal government.

On the contrary, you determined in the process of rebuilding to eliminate old conditions of which you were not proud; to build a better city; to replace congested areas with parks; to move human beings from slums to suburbs. For this you, the citizens of Gainesville, deserve all possible praise.

It is true that in the planned work of rebuilding you received federal assistance . . . But all of this would have been wholly insufficient if you had not provided far greater help from your own ranks in the form of money and in the form of unselfish cooperation. . . .

I tell you that this has a national significance and I want to give you a few illustrations of where and how the application of this principle to national problems would amply solve our national needs.

Today, national progress and national prosperity are being held back chiefly because of selfishness on the part of a few. If Gainesville had been faced with that type of minority selfishness your city would not stand rebuilt as it is today.

The type of selfishness to which I refer is definitely not to be applied to the overwhelming majority of the American public.

Most people, if they know both sides of a question and are appealed to, to support the public good, will gladly lay aside selfishness. But we must admit that there are some people who honestly believe in a wholly different theory of government than the one our Constitution provides.

You know their reasoning. They say that in the competition of life for the good things of life, "Some are successful because they have better brains or are more efficient; the wise, the swift, and the strong are able to outstrip their fellow men. That is nature itself, and it is just too bad if some get left behind."

It is that attitude which leads such people to give little thought to the one-third of our population which I have described as being ill-fed, ill-clad, and ill-housed. They say, "I am not my brother's keeper"—and they "pass by on the other side." Most of them are honest people. Most of them consider themselves excellent citizens.

But this nation will never permanently get on the road to recovery if we leave the methods and the processes of recovery to those who owned the government of the United States from 1921 to 1933.

They are the kind of people who, in 1936, were saying, "Oh, yes, we want nobody to starve"; but at the same time insisted that the balancing of the budget was more important than making appropriations for relief . . .

They have the same type of mind as those representatives of the people who vote against legislation to help social and economic conditions, proclaiming loudly that they are for the objectives but do not like the methods, and then fail utterly to offer a better method of their own.

I speak to you of conditions in this, my other state. The buying power of the people of Georgia and of the people of many other states is still so low today that the people of these states cannot purchase the products of industry. . . .

Mills and factories cannot sell to stores who have no customers.

I speak not only of the workers in the bottom third of our population . . . I speak also of millions of other workers who are so under-employed and so underpaid that the burden of their poverty affects the little business man and the big business man and the millionaire himself.

Georgia and the lower South may just as well face facts—simple facts. . . . The purchasing power of the millions of Americans in this whole area is far too low. Most men and women who work for wages in this whole area get wages which are far too low. . . .

And let us well remember that buying power means many other kinds of better things—better schools, better health, better hospitals, better highways. These things will not come to us in the South if we oppose progress—if we believe in our hearts that the feudal system is still the best system.

When you come down to it, there is little difference between the feudal system and the Fascist system. If you believe in the one, you lean to the other.

With the overwhelming majority of the people of this state, I oppose feudalism. So do many among those who by virtue of their circumstances in life belong to the most prosperous 5 percent of the population. Men and women in the professions, the overwhelming majority of the small storekeepers, a growing number of the bankers and business men—they are coming more and more to see that the continuation of the American system calls for the elimination of special privilege, the dissemination of the whole of the truth, and participation in prosperity by the people at the bottom of the ladder, as well as those in the middle and at the top.

One thing is certain—we are not going back to the old days. We are going forward to better days. We are calling for cooperation all along the line, and the cooperation is increasing because more and more people are coming to understand that abuses of the past which have been successfully eradicated are not going to be restored.

To those in and out of public office, who still believe in the feudal system—and believe in it honestly—the people of the United States and in every section of the United States are going to say "We are sorry, but we want people to represent us whose minds are cast in the 1938 mold and not in the 1898 mold."

The United States is rising and is rebuilding on sounder lines. We propose to go forward and not back.

25.

Remember That All of Us Are Descended from Immigrants and Revolutionists

Speech to the Daughters of the American Revolution
Washington, DC, April 21, 1938

In these extemporaneous remarks to the "white women only" members of the traditionally conservative Daughters of the American Revolution (DAR), Roosevelt sought to encourage them to a more multicultural understanding of what it means to be an American. But it was to little avail. Not long after, in 1939, First Lady Eleanor Roosevelt would resign from the DAR when it refused to permit the celebrated African American contralto Marian Anderson to perform before an integrated audience in Constitution Hall in Washington, DC. Notably, Mrs. Roosevelt then proceeded to help FDR's Secretary of the Interior, Harold Ickes, arrange what would become a famous performance by Ms. Anderson at the Lincoln Memorial on the National Mall.

. . . I have to ask you to bear with me, to let me just come here without preparation to tell you how glad I am to avail myself of this opportunity, to tell you how proud I am, as a Revolutionary descendant, to greet you.

I thought of preaching on a text, but I shall not. I shall only give you the text and I shall not preach on it. I think I can afford to give you the text because it so happens, through no fault of my own, that I am descended from a number of people who came over in the Mayflower. More than that, every one of my ancestors on both sides—and when you go back four generations or five generations it means thirty-two or sixty-four of them—every single one of them, without exception, was in this land in 1776. And there was only one Tory among them.

The text is this: Remember, remember always that all of us, and you and I especially, are descended from immigrants and revolutionists.

I am particularly glad to know that today you are making this fine appeal to the youth of America. . . .

We look for a younger generation that is going to be more American than we are. . . .

26.

If the Fires of Freedom and Civil Liberties Burn Low in Other Lands . . .

Speech to the National Education Association
New York City, June 30, 1938

Roosevelt stressed the role of education in building American democratic life, not only rhetorically, but also materially. Notably, the so-called Second New Deal included setting up the National Youth Administration, which, among other things, enabled young people to remain in high school by affording them work-study opportunities. In this speech to the National Education Association, FDR, after acknowledging the need to address educational inequalities nationally, urged teachers to defend freedom and democracy by not only upholding them, but also—in the face of the spread of Fascism overseas—seeking to advance them in thought and practice: "If the fires of freedom and civil liberties burn low in other lands, they must be made brighter in our own . . ."

Dr. Woodruff, Members of the National Education Association:

   . . . We have believed wholeheartedly in investing the money of all the people on the education of the people. That conviction, backed up by taxes and dollars, is no accident, for it is the logical application of our faith in democracy. . . .

   Here is where the whole problem of education ties in definitely with natural resources and the economic picture of the individual community or state. We all know that the best schools are, in most cases, located in those communities which can afford to spend the most money on them—the most money for adequate teachers' salaries, for modern buildings and for modern equipment of all kinds. We know that the weakest educational link in the system lies in those communities which have the lowest taxable values, therefore, the smallest per capita tax receipts and, therefore, the lowest teachers' salaries and most inadequate buildings and equipment. We do not blame these latter communities. They want better educational facilities, but simply have not enough money to pay the cost.

There is probably a wider divergence today in the standard of education between the richest communities and the poorest communities than there was one hundred years ago; and it is, therefore, our immediate task to seek to close that gap . . . We all know that if we do not close this gap it will continue to widen, for the best brains in the poor communities will either have no chance to develop or will migrate to those places where their ability will stand a better chance . . .

All of this leads me to ask you not to demand that the federal government provide financial assistance to all communities. Our aid for many reasons, financial and otherwise, must be confined to lifting the level at the bottom rather than to giving assistance at the top. Today we cannot do both, and we must therefore confine ourselves to the greater need.

In line with this policy, the federal government during the past five years has given relatively far more assistance to the poorer communities than to the rich. We have done it through direct relief and through work relief, through the Resettlement Administration and the Farm Security Administration, the National Youth Administration, and through the rehabilitation of flooded, stranded, or dust-blown areas. We have provided school houses, colleges, libraries, educational equipment, and sanitation in every state of the Union. I include "sanitation" because it has always seemed to me that good health and good education must go hand in hand. We have placed many millions of dollars in the field of adult education through the Works Progress Administration, and here, again, most of the money has been expended in the poorer communities of the land.

I have spoken of the twin interlocking assets of national and human resources and of the need of developing them hand in hand. But with this goes the equally important and equally difficult problem of keeping education intellectually free. For freedom to learn is the first necessity of guaranteeing that man himself shall be self-reliant enough to be free.

Such things did not need as much emphasis a generation ago; but when the clock of civilization can be turned back by burning libraries, by exiling scientists, artists, musicians, writers, and teachers, by dispersing universities, and by censoring news and literature and art, an added burden is placed upon those countries where the torch of free thought and free learning still burns bright.

If the fires of freedom and civil liberties burn low in other lands, they must be made brighter in our own.

If in other lands the press and books and literature of all kinds are censored, we must redouble our efforts here to keep them free.

If in other lands the eternal truths of the past are threatened by intolerance, we must provide a safe place for their perpetuation.

There may be times when men and women in the turmoil of change lose touch with the civilized gains of centuries of education; but the gains of education are never really lost. Books may be burned and cities sacked, but truth, like the yearning for freedom, lives in the hearts of humble men and women. The ultimate victory of tomorrow is with democracy, and through democracy with education, for no people in all the world can be kept eternally ignorant or eternally enslaved.

27.

Democracy Must Become a Positive Force in the Daily Lives of Its People

Radio Address in Favor of Voting for Liberals
Hyde Park, New York, November 4, 1938

In this speech on the eve of the 1938 midterm elections, Roosevelt called on Americans to vote for liberals. Deeply worried about the future progress of the New Deal due to the recent formation in Congress of a "conservative coalition" of Republicans and Southern Democrats, FDR warned (in words that remain relevant today): "As of today, Fascism and Communism—and old-line Tory Republicanism—are not threats to the continuation of our form of government. But I venture the challenging statement that if American democracy ceases to move forward as a living force, seeking day and night by peaceful means to better the lot of our citizens, then Fascism and Communism, aided, unconsciously perhaps, by old-line Tory Republicanism, will grow in strength in our land. . . ."

My friends:

On the eve of another election, I have come home to Hyde Park and am sitting at my own fireside in my own election district, my own county, and my own state. I have often expressed my feeling that the mere fact that I am president should not disqualify me from expressing as a citizen my views on candidates and issues in my own state. . . .

Democracy in order to live must become a positive force in the daily lives of its people. It must make men and women whose devotion it seeks feel that it really cares for the security of every individual; that it is tolerant enough to inspire an essential unity among its citizens; and that it is militant enough to maintain liberty against social oppression at home and against military aggression abroad.

The rest of the world is far closer to us in every way than in the days of democracy's founders—Jefferson, Jackson, and Lincoln. Comparisons in this world are unavoidable. To disprove the pretenses of rival systems, democracy must be an affirmative, up-to-date conception. It can no longer be negative—no longer adopt a defeatist attitude. In these tense and dangerous situations in the world, democracy will save itself with the average man and woman by proving itself worth saving.

Too many of those who prate about saving democracy are really only interested in saving things as they were. Democracy should concern itself also with things as they ought to be.

I am not talking mere idealism; I am expressing realistic necessity.

I reject the merely negative purposes proposed by old-line Republicans and Communists alike—for they are people whose only purpose is to survive against any other Fascist threat than their own.

As of today, Fascism and Communism—and old-line Tory Republicanism—are not threats to the continuation of our form of government. But I venture the challenging statement that if American democracy ceases to move forward as a living force, seeking day and night by peaceful means to better the lot of our citizens, then Fascism and Communism, aided, unconsciously perhaps, by old-line Tory Republicanism, will grow in strength in our land. . . .

There is no doubt of the basic desires of the American people. And because these basic desires are well known you find all parties, all candidates, making the same general promises to satisfy these desires.

During the weeks before a general election, all parties are the friends of labor, all parties are against monopoly, all parties say that the unemployed must have work or be given government relief, and all parties love the farmer.

Let me warn you now, as I warned you two years ago in my address at Syracuse, against the type of smooth evasion which says:

> "Of course we believe all these things; we believe in social security; we believe in work for the unemployed; we believe in saving homes. Cross our hearts and hope to die, we believe in all these things; but we do not like the way the present administration is doing them. Just turn them over to us. We will do all of them—we will do more of them—we will do them better; and, most important of all, the doing of them will not cost anybody anything."

But when democracy struggles for its very life, those same people obstruct our efforts to maintain it, while they fail to offer proof of their own will and their own plans to preserve it. They try to stop the only fire engine we have from rushing to the fire because they are sales agents for a different make of fire engine. . . .

Look over the rest of the names on the ballot next Tuesday. Pick those who are known for their experience and their liberalism. Pick them for what they have done, and not just for what they say they might do.

And one last but important word: Pick them without regard to race, color, or creed. Some of them may have come of the earliest Colonial stock; some of them may have been brought here as children to escape the tyrannies of the Old World. But remember that all of them are good American citizens now.

Remember that the Fathers of the American Revolution represented many religions and came from many foreign lands.

Remember that no matter what their origin they all agreed with Benjamin Franklin in that crisis: "We must indeed all hang together or most assuredly we shall all hang separately."

28.

Dictators Are Quick to Take Advantage of the Weakness of Others

Radio Address to a Forum on "Saving Democracy"
Washington, DC, October 24, 1940

Hitler's Nazi Propaganda Minister Joseph Goebbels would remark that "Nothing will be easier than to produce a bloody revolution in North America. No other country has so many social and racial tensions. . . . We shall be able to play on many strings there." In this radio address to the New York Herald Tribune *Forum on "Saving Democracy," FDR emphasized the need for American unity to withstand the efforts of fascists to exploit American's racial and religious divisions and subvert American democratic life: "It is the very mingling of races dedicated to common ideals which creates and recreates our vitality."*

Mrs. Reid, members of the *New York Herald Tribune* Forum:

In closing this Forum on the subject "Saving Democracy," I can think of no better text than the final words of the speech which Abraham Lincoln gave in Cooper Institute in New York City on February 27, 1860.

Lincoln was then speaking to an audience to whom he was a stranger. Represented in the audience, said the *New York Tribune* of that day, was the "intellect and moral culture" of the city. Lincoln warned them against the fearmongers and the calamity howlers—the "appeasers" of that troubled time, appeasers who were numerous and influential. He said:

> Neither let us be slandered from our duty by false accusations against us, nor frightened from it by menaces of destruction to the Government, nor of dungeons to ourselves. Let us have faith that right makes might, and in that faith let us to the end dare to do our duty as we understand it.

We do well to repeat Lincoln's declaration of faith today. It gives the right answer—the American answer—to the foreign propagandists who seek to divide us with their strategy of terror.

The repeaters of these slanders to our democracy, whether conscious disorganizers or unwitting dupes, seem to believe that if they tell us often enough that democracy is outworn and that we are decadent, we shall begin to believe it ourselves, and we shall immediately, obediently proceed to decay.

They have a strange misconception of our national character.

They believe, for one thing, that we Americans must be "hybrid, mongrel and undynamic"—so we are called by the enemies of democracy—because so many races have been fused together in our national community.

They believe we have no common tradition.

They believe that we are disunited and defenseless because we believe in free inquiries and free debate—because we argue with each other—because we engage in political campaigns—because we recognize the sacred right of the minority to disagree with the majority, and to express that disagreement, even loudly.

They believe that we are no match for a dictatorship in which uniformity is compulsory, in which each lives in terror of his neighbor and, worse still, in terror of himself, because the dominant atmosphere is that of the concentration camp.

Despising democracy and not knowing our strength, those who have destroyed other free peoples deem the United States an "effete, degenerate democracy."

At first we dismissed this contempt with our traditional spirit of good humor. We are now replying to it in characteristically American terms. We are preparing for the defense of the American continents, and of the oceans that are the highways of those two continents. And we are doing so in a mood of determination, but unafraid and resolute in our will to peace.

We are aware that the dictators are quick to take advantage of the weakness of others.

As to the humorless theory—that we are "hybrid and undynamic—mongrel and corrupt," and that, therefore, we can have no common tradition—let them look at most gatherings of Americans and study the common purpose that animates those gatherings. Let them look at any church sociable in any small town—at any fraternal convention, or meeting of doctors or mine workers—at any cheering section of any football game; let them look with especial attention at the crowds which will gather in and around every polling place on November fifth. Let them observe the unconquerable vitality of democracy. It is the very mingling of races dedicated to common ideals which creates and recreates our vitality.

In every representative American meeting there will be men and women and children with names like Jackson and Lincoln and Isaac and Schultz and O'Brien and Stuyvesant and Olson and Kovacs and Satori and Jones and Smith. These varied Americans with varied backgrounds are all immigrants or the descendants of immigrants. All of them are inheritors of the same stalwart tradition—a tradition of unusual enterprise, of adventurousness, of courage "to pull up stakes and git moving." That has been the great, compelling force in our history. Our continent, our hemisphere, has been populated by people who wanted a life better than the life they had previously known. They were willing to undergo all conceivable perils, all conceivable hardships, to achieve the better life. They were animated just as we are animated by this compelling force today. It is what makes us Americans.

The bold and the adventurous men, of many racial origins, were united in their determination to build a system which guaranteed freedom—for themselves and for all future generations. They built a system in which government and people are one—a nation which is a partnership—and can continue as a partnership.

That is our strength today.

The strength of every dictatorship depends upon the power of the one, almighty dictator—supported by a small, highly organized minority who call themselves the "elite."

We depend upon the power and allegiance of the one hundred and thirty million members of our national community from whom our government's authority is derived and to whom our government is forever responsible.

We gain in strength through progress—social, intellectual, and scientific. The more we perfect means of human communication between all parts of our community, the more united we become. Just as I, as elected head of your government, am privileged to talk to you over the radio, you talk to me. That is partnership. And it means that when, together, we make a decision, we act upon that decision as partners, and not in the inhuman manner of a capricious master toward his slaves.

The constant free flow of communication among us—enabling the free interchange of ideas—forms the very bloodstream of our nation. It keeps the mind and the body of our democracy eternally vital, eternally young.

We see, across the waters, that system undergoing a fearful test. Never before has a whole, free people been put to such a test. Never before have the citizens of a democracy—men and women and little children—displayed such courage, such unity, such strength of purpose, under appalling attack. Their homes and their schools, their churches and their national shrines, are being destroyed. But there is one mighty structure more enduring than marble, more precious than all that man has built, and that is the structure of the democratic faith.

We have confidence in the ability of the democratic system which gives men dignity, to give them strength. And so we say with Lincoln: "Let us have faith that right makes might, and in that faith let us to the end dare to do our duty as we understand it."

29.

We Are Characters in This Living Book of Democracy. But We Are Also Its Author

Campaign Address
Cleveland, Ohio, November 2, 1940

With World War II already under way in Europe and East Asia, Roosevelt ran for an unprecedented third term as president. In this stirring campaign speech, he not only rejected fascists' assertions that democracy had run its course and that fascism itself was the "wave of the future," but also celebrated what Americans themselves had accomplished democratically through their labors of the previous eight years of the New Deal and projected a vision of what they might yet accomplish democratically. Moreover, he evidently recognized that the "rendezvous with destiny" of which he had spoken in 1936 was fast approaching.

Mr. Chairman, ladies and gentlemen:

. . . For the past seven years I have had the high honor and the grave responsibility of leadership of the American people. In those seven years, the American people have marched forward, out of a wilderness of depression and despair.

They have marched forward right up to the very threshold of the future—a future which holds the fulfillment of our hopes for real freedom, real prosperity, real peace.

I want that march to continue for four more years. And for that purpose, I am asking your vote of confidence.

There are certain forces within our own national community, composed of men who call themselves American but who would destroy America. They are the forces of dictatorship in our land—on one hand, the Communists, and on the other, the Girdlers.

It is their constant purpose in this as in other lands to weaken democracy, to destroy the free man's faith in his own cause.

In this election all the representatives of those forces, without exception, are voting against the New Deal.

You and I are proud of that opposition. It is positive proof that what we have built and strengthened in the past seven years is democracy!

This generation of Americans is living in a tremendous moment of history.

The surge of events abroad has made some few doubters among us ask: Is this the end of a story that has been told? Is the book of democracy now to be closed and placed away upon the dusty shelves of time?

My answer is this: All we have known of the glories of democracy—its freedom, its efficiency as a mode of living, its ability to meet the aspirations of the common man—all these are merely an introduction to the greater story of a more glorious future.

We Americans of today—all of us—we are characters in this living book of democracy.

But we are also its author. It falls upon us now to say whether the chapters that are to come will tell a story of retreat or a story of continued advance.

I believe that the American people will say: "Forward!"

We look at the old world of Europe today. It is an ugly world, poisoned by hatred and greed and fear. We can see what has been the inevitable consequence of that poison—war.

We look at the country in which we live. It is a great country, built by generations of peaceable, friendly men and women who had in their hearts faith that the good life can be attained by those who will work for it.

We know that we are determined to defend our country—and with our neighbors to defend this hemisphere. We are strong in our defense. Every hour and every day we grow stronger.

Our foreign policy is shaped to express the determination of our government and the will of our people in our dealings with other nations. Those dealings, in the past few years, have been more difficult, more complex than ever before.

There is nothing secret about our foreign policy. It is not a secret from the American people—and it is not a secret from any government anywhere in the world. I have stated it many times before, not only in words but in action. Let me restate it like this:

The first purpose of our foreign policy is to keep our country out of war. At the same time, we seek to keep foreign conceptions of government out of the United States.

That is why we make ourselves strong; that is why we muster all the reserves of our national strength.

The second purpose of this policy is to keep war as far away as possible from the shores of the entire Western Hemisphere . . .

Finally, our policy is to give all possible material aid to the nations which still resist aggression, across the Atlantic and Pacific Oceans.

And let me make it perfectly clear that we intend to commit none of the fatal errors of appeasement.

We in this nation of many states have found the way by which men of many racial origins may live together in peace.

If the human race as a whole is to survive, the world must find the way by which men and nations can live together in peace. We cannot accept the doctrine that war must be forever a part of man's destiny.

We do know what would be the foreign policy of those who are doubters about our democracy.

We do not know what would be the foreign policy of those who are obviously trying to sit on both sides of the fence at the same time. Ours is the foreign policy of an administration which has undying faith in the strength of our democracy today, full confidence in the vitality of our democracy in the future, and a consistent record in the cause of peace.

Our strength is measured not only in terms of the might of our armaments. It is measured not only in terms of the horsepower of our machines.

The true measure of our strength lies deeply imbedded in the social and economic justice of the system in which we live.

For you can build ships and tanks and planes and guns galore; but they will not be enough. You must place behind them an invincible faith in the institutions which they have been built to defend.

The dictators have devised a new system—or, rather, a modern, streamlined version of a very ancient system.

But Americans will have none of that. They will never submit to domination or influence by Nazism or Communism. They will hesitate to support those of whom they are not absolutely sure.

For Americans are determined to retain for themselves the right of free speech, free religion, free assembly, and the right which lies at the basis of all of them—the right to choose the officers of their own government in free elections.

We intend to keep our freedom—to defend it from attacks from without and against corruption from within. We shall defend it against the forces of dictatorship, whatever disguises and false faces they may wear.

But we have learned that freedom in itself is not enough.

Freedom of speech is of no use to a man who has nothing to say.

Freedom of worship is of no use to a man who has lost his God.

Democracy, to be dynamic, must provide for its citizens opportunity as well as freedom.

We of this generation have seen a rebirth of dynamic democracy in America in these past few years.

The American people have faced with courage the most severe problems of all of our modern history.

The start toward a solution of these problems had to be made seven years ago by providing the bare necessities of life—food and shelter and clothing. The American people insisted that those obligations were a concern of government; they denied that the only solution was the poorhouse.

Your government assumed its proper function as the working representative of the average men and women of America. And the reforms in our social structure that we have achieved these permanent reforms are your achievement.

The New Deal has been the creation of you, the American people.

You provided work for free men and women in America who could find no work . . .

You used the powers of government to stop the depletion of the topsoil of America, to stop decline in farm prices, to stop foreclosures of homes and farms.

You wrote into the law the right of working men and women to bargain collectively, and you set up the machinery to enforce that right.

You turned to the problems of youth and age. You took your children out of the factory and shop and outlawed the right of anyone to exploit the labor of those children; and you gave to those children the chance to prepare in body and spirit the molding of an even fuller and brighter day for themselves. For the youth of the land you provided chances for jobs and for education. And for old age itself you provided security and rest.

You made safe the banks which held your savings. You stopped, once and for all, gambling with other people's money—money changing in the temple.

You advanced to other objectives. You gained them, you consolidated them and advanced again. . . .

Now we are asked to stop in our tracks. We are asked to turn about, to march back into the wilderness from which we came.

Of course we will not turn backward. We will not turn back because we are the inheritors of a tradition of pioneering, exploring, experimenting and adventuring. We will not be scared into retreating by threats from the doubters of democracy. . . .

Of course we shall continue to strengthen all these dynamic reforms in our social and economic life; to keep the processes of democracy side by side with the necessities and possibilities of modern industrial production.

Of course we shall continue to make available the good things of life created by the genius of science and technology—to use them, however, not for the enjoyment of the few but for the welfare of all.

For there lies the road to democracy that is strong.

Of course we intend to preserve and build up the land of this country—its soil, its forests, and its rivers—all the resources with which God has endowed the people of the United States.

Of course we intend to continue to build up the bodies and the minds of the men, women, and children of the nation—through democratic education and a democratic program for health.

For there lies the road to democracy that is strong.

Of course we intend to continue our efforts to protect our system of private enterprise and private property, but to protect it from monopoly of financial control on the one hand and from Communistic wrecking on the other.

Of course we shall continue our efforts to prevent economic dictatorship as well as political dictatorship.

Of course we intend to continue to build up the morale of this country, not as blind obedience to some leader, but as the expression of confidence in the deeply ethical principles upon which this nation and its democracy were founded.

For there lies the road to democracy that is strong.

The progress of our country, as well as the defense of our country, requires national unity . . .

And all the forces of evil shall not prevail against it.

For so it is written in the Book, and so it is written in the moral law, and so it is written in the promise of a great era of world peace.

This nation which is arming itself for defense has also the intelligence to save its human resources by giving them that confidence which comes from useful work. . . .

It is the destiny of this American generation to point the road to the future for all the world to see. It is our prayer that all lovers of freedom may join us—the anguished common people of this earth for whom we seek to light the path.

I see an America where factory workers are not discarded after they reach their prime, where there is no endless chain of poverty from generation to generation, where impoverished farmers and farm hands do not become homeless wanderers, where monopoly does not make youth a beggar for a job.

I see an America whose rivers and valleys and lakes—hills and streams and plains—the mountains over our land and nature's wealth deep under the earth—are protected as the rightful heritage of all the people.

I see an America where small business really has a chance to flourish and grow.

I see an America of great cultural and educational opportunity for all its people.

I see an America where the income from the land shall be implemented and protected by a government determined to guarantee to those who hoe it a fair share in the national income.

An America where the wheels of trade and private industry continue to turn to make the goods for America. Where no businessman can be stifled by the harsh hand of monopoly, and where the legitimate profits of legitimate business are the fair reward of every businessman—big and little—in all the nation.

I see an America with peace in the ranks of labor.

An America where the workers are really free and—through their great unions undominated by any outside force, or by any dictator within—can take their proper place at the council table with the owners and managers of business. Where the dignity and security of the working man and woman are guaranteed by their own strength and fortified by the safeguards of law.

An America where those who have reached the evening of life shall live out their years in peace and security. Where pensions and insurance for these aged shall be given as a matter of right to those who through a long life of labor have served their families and their nation as well.

I see an America devoted to our freedom—unified by tolerance and by religious faith—a people consecrated to peace, a people confident in strength because their body and their spirit are secure and unafraid. . . .

During these years while our democracy advanced on many fields of battle, I have had the great privilege of being your president. No personal ambition of any man could desire more than that. . . .

There is a great storm raging now, a storm that makes things harder for the world. And that storm, which did not start in this land of ours, is the true reason that I would like to stick by these people of ours until we reach the clear, sure footing ahead.

We will make it—we will make it before the next term is over.

We will make it; and the world, we hope, will make it, too. . . .

Our future belongs to us Americans.

The spirit of the common man is the spirit of peace and good will. It is the spirit of God. And in His faith is the strength of all America.

30.

We Must Be the Great Arsenal of Democracy

Fireside Chat
Washington, DC, December 29, 1940

In November 1940, FDR was elected to a third term as president. Meanwhile, the United Kingdom was under siege by Nazi Germany and facing the possibility of a German invasion. In this Fireside Chat, Roosevelt spoke directly to the danger of Hitler conquering all of Europe and the urgent need for the United States to transform itself into the Arsenal of Democracy—not only to prepare the United States to defend itself, but also to provide Britain with the wherewithal to continue to defend itself against the Nazis.

My friends:

This is not a fireside chat on war. It is a talk on national security; because the nub of the whole purpose of your president is to keep you now, and your children later, and your grandchildren much later, out of a last-ditch war for the preservation of American independence and all the things that American independence means to you and to me and to ours.

Tonight, in the presence of a world crisis, my mind goes back eight years to a night in the midst of a domestic crisis. It was a time when the wheels of American industry were grinding to a full stop, when the whole banking system of our country had ceased to function.

I well remember that while I sat in my study in the White House, preparing to talk with the people of the United States, I had before my eyes the picture of all those Americans with whom I was talking. I saw the workmen in the mills, the mines, the factories; the girl behind the counter; the small shopkeeper; the farmer doing his spring plowing; the widows and the old men wondering about their life's savings.

I tried to convey to the great mass of American people what the banking crisis meant to them in their daily lives.

Tonight, I want to do the same thing, with the same people, in this new crisis which faces America. We met the issue of 1933 with courage and realism.

We face this new crisis—this new threat to the security of our nation—with the same courage and realism.

Never before since Jamestown and Plymouth Rock has our American civilization been in such danger as now.

For, on September 27, 1940, by an agreement signed in Berlin, three powerful nations, two in Europe and one in Asia, joined themselves together in the threat that if the United States of America interfered with or blocked the expansion program of these three nations—a program aimed at world control—they would unite in ultimate action against the United States.

The Nazi masters of Germany have made it clear that they intend not only to dominate all life and thought in their own country, but also to enslave the whole of Europe, and then to use the resources of Europe to dominate the rest of the world.

It was only three weeks ago their leader stated this: "There are two worlds that stand opposed to each other." And then in defiant reply to his opponents, he said this: "Others are correct when they say: With this world we cannot ever reconcile ourselves. . . . I can beat any other power in the world." So said the leader of the Nazis.

In other words, the Axis not merely admits but proclaims that there can be no ultimate peace between their philosophy of government and our philosophy of government.

In view of the nature of this undeniable threat, it can be asserted, properly and categorically, that the United States has no right or reason to encourage talk of peace, until the day shall come when there is a clear intention on the part of the aggressor nations to abandon all thought of dominating or conquering the world. . . .

Some of our people like to believe that wars in Europe and in Asia are of no concern to us. But it is a matter of most vital concern to us that European and Asiatic war-makers should not gain control of the oceans which lead to this hemisphere. . . .

If Great Britain goes down, the Axis powers will control the continents of Europe, Asia, Africa, Australasia, and the high seas—and they will be in a position to bring enormous military and naval resources against this hemisphere. It is no exaggeration to say that all of us, in all the Americas, would be living at the point of a gun—a gun loaded with explosive bullets, economic as well as military. . . .

Let us no longer blind ourselves to the undeniable fact that the evil forces which have crushed and undermined and corrupted so many others are already within our own gates. Your government knows much about them and every day is ferreting them out.

Their secret emissaries are active in our own and in neighboring countries. They seek to stir up suspicion and dissension to cause internal strife. They try to turn capital against labor, and vice versa. They try to reawaken long-slumbering racial and religious enmities which should have no place in this country. They are active in every group that promotes intolerance. They exploit for their own ends our natural abhorrence of war. These trouble-breeders have but one purpose. It is to divide our people into hostile groups and to destroy our unity and shatter our will to defend ourselves.

There are also American citizens, many of them in high places, who, unwittingly in most cases, are aiding and abetting the work of these agents. I do not charge these American citizens with being foreign agents. But I do charge them with doing exactly the kind of work that the dictators want done in the United States.

These people not only believe that we can save our own skins by shutting our eyes to the fate of other nations. Some of them go much further than that. They say that we can and should become the friends and even the partners of the Axis powers. Some of them even suggest that we should imitate the methods of the dictatorships. Americans never can and never will do that.

The experience of the past two years has proven beyond doubt that no nation can appease the Nazis. No man can tame a tiger into a kitten by stroking it. There can be no appeasement with ruthlessness. There can be no reasoning with an incendiary bomb. We know now that a nation can have peace with the Nazis only at the price of total surrender. . . .

The American appeasers ignore the warning to be found in the fate of Austria, Czechoslovakia, Poland, Norway, Belgium, the Netherlands, Denmark, and France. They tell you that the Axis powers are going to win anyway; that all this bloodshed in the world could be saved; that the United States might just as well throw its influence into the scale of a dictated peace, and get the best out of it that we can.

They call it a "negotiated peace." Nonsense! Is it a negotiated peace if a gang of outlaws surrounds your community and on threat of extermination makes you pay tribute to save your own skins?

Such a dictated peace would be no peace at all. It would be only another armistice, leading to the most gigantic armament race and the most devastating trade wars in all history. And in these contests the Americas would offer the only real resistance to the Axis powers.

With all their vaunted efficiency, with all their parade of pious purpose in this war, there are still in their background the concentration camp and the servants of God in chains.

The history of recent years proves that shootings and chains and concentration camps are not simply the transient tools but the very altars of modern dictatorships. They may talk of a "new order" in the world, but what they have in mind is only a revival of the oldest and the worst tyranny. In that there is no liberty, no religion, no hope.

The proposed "new order" is the very opposite of a United States of Europe or a United States of Asia. It is not a government based upon the consent of the governed. It is not a union of ordinary, self-respecting men and women to protect themselves and their freedom and their dignity from oppression. It is an unholy alliance of power and pelf to dominate and enslave the human race.

The British people and their allies today are conducting an active war against this unholy alliance. Our own future security is greatly dependent on the outcome of that fight. Our ability to "keep out of war" is going to be affected by that outcome.

Thinking in terms of today and tomorrow, I make the direct statement to the American people that there is far less chance of the United States getting into war, if we do all we can now to support the nations defending themselves against attack by the Axis than if we acquiesce in their defeat, submit tamely to an Axis victory, and wait our turn to be the object of attack in another war later on.

If we are to be completely honest with ourselves, we must admit that there is risk in any course we may take. But I deeply believe that the great majority of our people agree that the course that I advocate involves the least risk now and the greatest hope for world peace in the future.

The people of Europe who are defending themselves do not ask us to do their fighting. They ask us for the implements of war, the planes, the tanks, the guns, the freighters which will enable them to fight for their liberty and for our security. Emphatically we must get these weapons to them in sufficient volume and quickly enough so that we and our children will be saved the agony and suffering of war which others have had to endure.

Let not the defeatists tell us that it is too late. It will never be earlier. Tomorrow will be later than today. Certain facts are self-evident.

In a military sense Great Britain and the British Empire are today the spearhead of resistance to world conquest. They are putting up a fight which will live forever in the story of human gallantry.

There is no demand for sending an American Expeditionary Force outside our own borders. There is no intention by any member of your government to send such a force. You can, therefore, nail any talk about sending armies to Europe as deliberate untruth.

Our national policy is not directed toward war. Its sole purpose is to keep war away from our country and our people.

Democracy's fight against world conquest is being greatly aided, and must be more greatly aided, by the rearmament of the United States and by sending every ounce and every ton of munitions and supplies that we can possibly spare to help the defenders who are in the front lines. . . .

We are planning our own defense with the utmost urgency; and in its vast scale we must integrate the war needs of Britain and the other free nations which are resisting aggression.

This is not a matter of sentiment or of controversial personal opinion. It is a matter of realistic, practical military policy, based on the advice of our military experts who are in close touch with existing warfare. These military and naval experts and the members of the Congress and the administration have a single-minded purpose—the defense of the United States.

This nation is making a great effort to produce everything that is necessary in this emergency—and with all possible speed. This great effort requires great sacrifice.

I would ask no one to defend a democracy which in turn would not defend everyone in the nation against want and privation. The strength of this nation shall not be diluted by the failure of the government to protect the economic well-being of its citizens.

If our capacity to produce is limited by machines, it must ever be remembered that these machines are operated by the skill and the stamina of the workers. As the government is determined to protect the rights of the workers, so the nation has a right to expect that the men who man the machines will discharge their full responsibilities to the urgent needs of defense.

The worker possesses the same human dignity and is entitled to the same security of position as the engineer or the manager or the owner. For the workers provide the human power that turns out the destroyers, the airplanes, and the tanks.

The nation expects our defense industries to continue operation without interruption by strikes or lock-outs. It expects and insists that management and workers will reconcile their differences by voluntary or legal means, to continue to produce the supplies that are so sorely needed. . . .

In this great work there has been splendid cooperation between the government and industry and labor; and I am very thankful. . . .

I want to make it clear that it is the purpose of the nation to build now with all possible speed every machine, every arsenal, every factory that we need to manufacture our defense material. We have the men—the skill— the wealth—and above all, the will.

I am confident that if and when production of consumer or luxury goods in certain industries requires the use of machines and raw materials that are essential for defense purposes, then such production must yield, and will gladly yield, to our primary and compelling purpose.

I appeal to the owners of plants—to the managers—to the workers—to our own government employees—to put every ounce of effort into producing these munitions swiftly and without stint. With this appeal I give you the pledge that all of us who are officers of your government will devote ourselves to the same wholehearted extent to the great task that lies ahead. . . .

We must be the great arsenal of democracy. For us this is an emergency as serious as war itself. We must apply ourselves to our task with the same resolution, the same sense of urgency, the same spirit of patriotism and sacrifice as we would show were we at war. . . .

31.

We Look Forward to a World Founded Upon Four Essential Human Freedoms

Annual Message to Congress
Washington, DC, January 6, 1941

Only one week after his "Arsenal of Democracy" Fireside Chat, Roosevelt delivered his 1941 Annual Message to Congress. Speaking again of the Nazi and fascist threat, he made it clear that the dictatorships would likely attack the United States itself. But notably, as much as he urged turning the economy into the Arsenal of Democracy, he also insisted that doing so did not mean the country should suspend or give up the advances of the New Deal, which many a Republican was demanding. Indeed, he insisted that a strong defense required pursuing the programs of economic and social reform all the more aggressively. Finally, with America's own historic promise in mind, he offered a vision, a promise, of a postwar world founded upon the Four Freedoms—freedom of speech and expression, freedom of worship, freedom from want, and freedom from fear—which would become the theme of America's ensuing war effort.

Mr. President, Mr. Speaker, members of the Seventy-seventh Congress:

I address you, the members of the Seventy-seventh Congress, at a moment unprecedented in the history of the Union. I use the word "unprecedented," because at no previous time has American security been as seriously threatened from without as it is today.

Since the permanent formation of our government under the Constitution, in 1789, most of the periods of crisis in our history have related to our domestic affairs. Fortunately, only one of these—the four-year War Between the States—ever threatened our national unity. Today, thank God, one hundred and thirty million Americans, in forty-eight states, have forgotten points of the compass in our national unity.

It is true that prior to 1914 the United States often had been disturbed by events in other continents. We had even engaged in two wars with

European nations and in a number of undeclared wars in the West Indies, in the Mediterranean, and in the Pacific for the maintenance of American rights and for the principles of peaceful commerce. But in no case had a serious threat been raised against our national safety or our continued independence.

What I seek to convey is the historic truth that the United States as a nation has at all times maintained clear, definite opposition to any attempt to lock us in behind an ancient Chinese wall while the procession of civilization went past. Today, thinking of our children and of their children, we oppose enforced isolation for ourselves or for any other part of the Americas.

That determination of ours, extending over all these years, was proved, for example, during the quarter century of wars following the French Revolution.

While the Napoleonic struggles did threaten interests of the United States because of the French foothold in the West Indies and in Louisiana, and while we engaged in the War of 1812 to vindicate our right to peaceful trade, it is nevertheless clear that neither France nor Great Britain, nor any other nation, was aiming at domination of the whole world.

In like fashion from 1815 to 1914—ninety-nine years—no single war in Europe or in Asia constituted a real threat against our future or against the future of any other American nation.

Except in the Maximilian interlude in Mexico, no foreign power sought to establish itself in this hemisphere; and the strength of the British fleet in the Atlantic has been a friendly strength. It is still a friendly strength.

Even when the World War broke out in 1914, it seemed to contain only small threat of danger to our own American future. But as time went on, the American people began to visualize what the downfall of democratic nations might mean to our own democracy.

We need not overemphasize imperfections in the Peace of Versailles. We need not harp on failure of the democracies to deal with problems of world reconstruction. We should remember that the Peace of 1919 was far less unjust than the kind of "pacification" which began even before Munich, and which is being carried on under the new order of tyranny that seeks to spread over every continent today. The American people have unalterably set their faces against that tyranny.

Every realist knows that the democratic way of life is at this moment being directly assailed in every part of the world—assailed either by arms, or by secret spreading of poisonous propaganda by those who seek to destroy unity and promote discord in nations that are still at peace.

During sixteen long months this assault has blotted out the whole pattern of democratic life in an appalling number of independent nations, great and small. The assailants are still on the march, threatening other nations, great and small.

Therefore, as your president, performing my constitutional duty to "give to the Congress information of the state of the Union," I find it, unhappily, necessary to report that the future and the safety of our country and of our democracy are overwhelmingly involved in events far beyond our borders.

Armed defense of democratic existence is now being gallantly waged in four continents. If that defense fails, all the population and all the resources of Europe, Asia, Africa, and Australasia will be dominated by the conquerors. Let us remember that the total of those populations and their resources in those four continents greatly exceeds the sum total of the population and the resources of the whole of the Western Hemisphere—many times over.

In times like these it is immature—and, incidentally, untrue—for anybody to brag that an unprepared America, single-handed, and with one hand tied behind its back, can hold off the whole world.

No realistic American can expect from a dictator's peace international generosity, or return of true independence, or world disarmament, or freedom of expression, or freedom of religion—or even good business.

Such a peace would bring no security for us or for our neighbors. "Those who would give up essential liberty to purchase a little temporary safety, deserve neither liberty nor safety."

As a nation, we may take pride in the fact that we are softhearted; but we cannot afford to be soft-headed.

We must always be wary of those who with sounding brass and a tinkling cymbal preach the "ism" of appeasement.

We must especially beware of that small group of selfish men who would clip the wings of the American eagle in order to feather their own nests.

I have recently pointed out how quickly the tempo of modern warfare could bring into our very midst the physical attack which we must eventually expect if the dictator nations win this war.

There is much loose talk of our immunity from immediate and direct invasion from across the seas. Obviously, as long as the British Navy retains its power, no such danger exists. Even if there were no British Navy, it is not probable that any enemy would be stupid enough to attack us by landing troops in the United States from across thousands of miles of ocean, until it had acquired strategic bases from which to operate.

But we learn much from the lessons of the past years in Europe—particularly the lesson of Norway, whose essential seaports were captured by treachery and surprise built up over a series of years.

The first phase of the invasion of this hemisphere would not be the landing of regular troops. The necessary strategic points would be occupied by secret agents and their dupes—and great numbers of them are already here, and in Latin America.

As long as the aggressor nations maintain the offensive, they—not we—will choose the time and the place and the method of their attack.

That is why the future of all the American Republics is today in serious danger.

That is why this Annual Message to the Congress is unique in our history.

That is why every member of the executive branch of the government and every member of the Congress faces great responsibility and great accountability.

The need of the moment is that our actions and our policy should be devoted primarily—almost exclusively—to meeting this foreign peril. For all our domestic problems are now a part of the great emergency.

Just as our national policy in internal affairs has been based upon a decent respect for the rights and the dignity of all our fellow men within our gates, so our national policy in foreign affairs has been based on a decent respect for the rights and dignity of all nations, large and small. And the justice of morality must and will win in the end.

Our national policy is this:

First, by an impressive expression of the public will and without regard to partisanship, we are committed to all-inclusive national defense.

Second, by an impressive expression of the public will and without regard to partisanship, we are committed to full support of all those resolute peoples, everywhere, who are resisting aggression and are thereby keeping war away from our hemisphere. By this support, we express our determination that the democratic cause shall prevail; and we strengthen the defense and the security of our own nation.

Third, by an impressive expression of the public will and without regard to partisanship, we are committed to the proposition that principles of morality and considerations for our own security will never permit us to acquiesce in a peace dictated by aggressors and sponsored by appeasers. We know that enduring peace cannot be bought at the cost of other people's freedom.

In the recent national election there was no substantial difference between the two great parties in respect to that national policy. No issue was fought out on this line before the American electorate. Today it is abundantly evident that American citizens everywhere are demanding and supporting speedy and complete action in recognition of obvious danger.

Therefore, the immediate need is a swift and driving increase in our armament production. . . .

I am not satisfied with the progress thus far made. The men in charge of the program represent the best in training, in ability, and in patriotism. They are not satisfied with the progress thus far made. None of us will be satisfied until the job is done. . . .

To change a whole nation from a basis of peacetime production of implements of peace to a basis of wartime production of implements of war is no small task. And the greatest difficulty comes at the beginning of the program, when new tools, new plant facilities, new assembly lines, and new shipways must first be constructed before the actual materiel begins to flow steadily and speedily from them.

The Congress, of course, must rightly keep itself informed at all times of the progress of the program. However, there is certain information, as the Congress itself will readily recognize, which, in the interests of our own security and those of the nations that we are supporting, must of needs be kept in confidence.

New circumstances are constantly begetting new needs for our safety. I shall ask this Congress for greatly increased new appropriations and authorizations to carry on what we have begun.

I also ask this Congress for authority and for funds sufficient to manufacture additional munitions and war supplies of many kinds, to be turned over to those nations which are now in actual war with aggressor nations.

Our most useful and immediate role is to act as an arsenal for them as well as for ourselves. They do not need manpower, but they do need billions of dollars' worth of the weapons of defense.

The time is near when they will not be able to pay for them all in ready cash. We cannot, and we will not, tell them that they must surrender, merely because of present inability to pay for the weapons which we know they must have.

I do not recommend that we make them a loan of dollars with which to pay for these weapons—a loan to be repaid in dollars.

I recommend that we make it possible for those nations to continue to obtain war materials in the United States, fitting their orders into our own program. Nearly all their materiel would, if the time ever came, be useful for our own defense.

Taking counsel of expert military and naval authorities, considering what is best for our own security, we are free to decide how much should be kept here and how much should be sent abroad to our friends who by their determined and heroic resistance are giving us time in which to make ready our own defense.

For what we send abroad, we shall be repaid within a reasonable time following the close of hostilities, in similar materials, or, at our option, in other goods of many kinds, which they can produce and which we need.

Let us say to the democracies: "We Americans are vitally concerned in your defense of freedom. We are putting forth our energies, our resources and our organizing powers to give you the strength to regain and maintain a free world. We shall send you, in ever-increasing numbers, ships, planes, tanks, guns. This is our purpose and our pledge."

In fulfillment of this purpose we will not be intimidated by the threats of dictators that they will regard as a breach of international law or as an act of war our aid to the democracies which dare to resist their aggression. Such aid is not an act of war, even if a dictator should unilaterally proclaim it so to be.

When the dictators, if the dictators, are ready to make war upon us, they will not wait for an act of war on our part. They did not wait for Norway or Belgium or the Netherlands to commit an act of war.

Their only interest is in a new one-way international law, which lacks mutuality in its observance, and, therefore, becomes an instrument of oppression.

The happiness of future generations of Americans may well depend upon how effective and how immediate we can make our aid felt. No one can tell the exact character of the emergency situations that we may be called upon to meet. The nation's hands must not be tied when the nation's life is in danger.

We must all prepare to make the sacrifices that the emergency—almost as serious as war itself—demands. Whatever stands in the way of speed and efficiency in defense preparations must give way to the national need.

A free nation has the right to expect full cooperation from all groups. A free nation has the right to look to the leaders of business, of labor, and of agriculture to take the lead in stimulating effort, not among other groups but within their own groups.

The best way of dealing with the few slackers or troublemakers in our midst is, first, to shame them by patriotic example, and, if that fails, to use the sovereignty of government to save government.

As men do not live by bread alone, they do not fight by armaments alone. Those who man our defenses, and those behind them who build our defenses, must have the stamina and the courage which come from unshakable belief in the manner of life which they are defending. The mighty action that we are calling for cannot be based on a disregard of all things worth fighting for.

The nation takes great satisfaction and much strength from the things which have been done to make its people conscious of their individual stake in the preservation of democratic life in America. Those things have toughened the fiber of our people, have renewed their faith and strengthened their devotion to the institutions we make ready to protect.

Certainly this is no time for any of us to stop thinking about the social and economic problems which are the root cause of the social revolution which is today a supreme factor in the world.

For there is nothing mysterious about the foundations of a healthy and strong democracy. The basic things expected by our people of their political and economic systems are simple. They are:

Equality of opportunity for youth and for others.

Jobs for those who can work.

Security for those who need it.

The ending of special privilege for the few.

The preservation of civil liberties for all.

The enjoyment of the fruits of scientific progress in a wider and constantly rising standard of living.

These are the simple, basic things that must never be lost sight of in the turmoil and unbelievable complexity of our modern world. The inner and abiding strength of our economic and political systems is dependent upon the degree to which they fulfill these expectations.

Many subjects connected with our social economy call for immediate improvement.

As examples:

We should bring more citizens under the coverage of old-age pensions and unemployment insurance.

We should widen the opportunities for adequate medical care.

We should plan a better system by which persons deserving or needing gainful employment may obtain it.

I have called for personal sacrifice. I am assured of the willingness of almost all Americans to respond to that call.

A part of the sacrifice means the payment of more money in taxes. In my Budget Message I shall recommend that a greater portion of this great defense program be paid for from taxation than we are paying today. No person should try, or be allowed, to get rich out of this program; and the principle of tax payments in accordance with ability to pay should be constantly before our eyes to guide our legislation.

If the Congress maintains these principles, the voters, putting patriotism ahead of pocketbooks, will give you their applause.

In the future days, which we seek to make secure, we look forward to a world founded upon four essential human freedoms.

The first is freedom of speech and expression—everywhere in the world.

The second is freedom of every person to worship God in his own way—everywhere in the world.

The third is freedom from want—which, translated into world terms, means economic understandings which will secure to every nation a healthy peacetime life for its inhabitants—everywhere in the world.

The fourth is freedom from fear—which, translated into world terms, means a world-wide reduction of armaments to such a point and in such a thorough fashion that no nation will be in a position to commit an act of physical aggression against any neighbor—anywhere in the world.

That is no vision of a distant millennium. It is a definite basis for a kind of world attainable in our own time and generation. That kind of world is the very antithesis of the so-called new order of tyranny which the dictators seek to create with the crash of a bomb.

To that new order we oppose the greater conception—the moral order. A good society is able to face schemes of world domination and foreign revolutions alike without fear.

Since the beginning of our American history, we have been engaged in change—in a perpetual peaceful revolution—a revolution which goes on steadily, quietly adjusting itself to changing conditions—without the concentration camp or the quick-lime in the ditch. The world order which we seek is the cooperation of free countries, working together in a friendly, civilized society.

This nation has placed its destiny in the hands and heads and hearts of its millions of free men and women; and its faith in freedom under the guidance of God. Freedom means the supremacy of human rights everywhere. Our support goes to those who struggle to gain those rights or keep them. Our strength is our unity of purpose.

To that high concept there can be no end save victory.

PART III

Third and Fourth Presidential Terms
(1941–1945)

32.

Our Strong Purpose Is to Protect and Perpetuate the Integrity of Democracy

Third Inaugural Address
Washington, DC, January 20, 1941

In his third inaugural address, Roosevelt—citing the nation's great wartime leaders of the past, George Washington and Abraham Lincoln—once again reached back into American history to remind Americans of who they were and what the struggle ahead was truly about: the defense of democracy.

On each national day of inauguration since 1789, the people have renewed their sense of dedication to the United States.

In Washington's day the task of the people was to create and weld together a nation.

In Lincoln's day the task of the people was to preserve that nation from disruption from within.

In this day the task of the people is to save that nation and its institutions from disruption from without.

To us there has come a time, in the midst of swift happenings, to pause for a moment and take stock—to recall what our place in history has been, and to rediscover what we are and what we may be. If we do not, we risk the real peril of isolation, the real peril of inaction.

Lives of nations are determined not by the count of years, but by the lifetime of the human spirit. The life of a man is threescore years and ten: a little more, a little less. The life of a nation is the fullness of the measure of its will to live.

There are men who doubt this. There are men who believe that democracy, as a form of government and a frame of life, is limited or measured by a kind of mystical and artificial fate that, for some unexplained reason, tyranny and slavery have become the surging wave of the future—and that freedom is an ebbing tide.

But we Americans know that this is not true.

Eight years ago, when the life of this Republic seemed frozen by a fatalistic terror, we proved that this is not true. We were in the midst of shock—but we acted. We acted quickly, boldly, decisively.

These later years have been living years—fruitful years for the people of this democracy. For they have brought to us greater security and, I hope, a better understanding that life's ideals are to be measured in other than material things.

Most vital to our present and to our future is this experience of a democracy which successfully survived crisis at home; put away many evil things; built new structures on enduring lines; and, through it all, maintained the fact of its democracy.

For action has been taken within the three-way framework of the Constitution of the United States. The coordinate branches of the government continue freely to function. The Bill of Rights remains inviolate. The freedom of elections is wholly maintained. Prophets of the downfall of American democracy have seen their dire predictions come to naught.

No, democracy is not dying.

We know it because we have seen it revive—and grow.

We know it cannot die—because it is built on the unhampered initiative of individual men and women joined together in a common enterprise—an enterprise undertaken and carried through by the free expression of a free majority.

We know it because democracy alone, of all forms of government, enlists the full force of men's enlightened will.

We know it because democracy alone has constructed an unlimited civilization capable of infinite progress in the improvement of human life.

We know it because, if we look below the surface, we sense it still spreading on every continent—for it is the most humane, the most advanced, and in the end the most unconquerable of all forms of human society.

A nation, like a person, has a body—a body that must be fed and clothed and housed, invigorated and rested, in a manner that measures up to the standards of our time.

A nation, like a person, has a mind—a mind that must be kept informed and alert, that must know itself, that understands the hopes and the needs of its neighbors—all the other nations that live within the narrowing circle of the world.

A nation, like a person, has something deeper, something more permanent, something larger than the sum of all its parts. It is that something which matters most to its future—which calls forth the most sacred guarding of its present.

It is a thing for which we find it difficult—even impossible—to hit upon a single, simple word.

And yet, we all understand what it is—the spirit—the faith of America. It is the product of centuries. It was born in the multitudes of those who came from many lands—some of high degree, but mostly plain people—who sought here, early and late, to find freedom more freely.

The democratic aspiration is no mere recent phase in human history. It is human history. It permeated the ancient life of early peoples. It blazed anew in the Middle Ages. It was written in Magna Carta.

In the Americas its impact has been irresistible. America has been the New World in all tongues, and to all peoples, not because this continent was a new-found land, but because all those who came here believed they could create upon this continent a new life—a life that should be new in freedom.

Its vitality was written into our own Mayflower Compact, into the Declaration of Independence, into the Constitution of the United States, into the Gettysburg Address.

Those who first came here to carry out the longings of their spirit, and the millions who followed, and the stock that sprang from them—all have moved forward constantly and consistently toward an ideal which in itself has gained stature and clarity with each generation.

The hopes of the Republic cannot forever tolerate either undeserved poverty or self-serving wealth.

We know that we still have far to go; that we must more greatly build the security and the opportunity and the knowledge of every citizen, in the measure justified by the resources and the capacity of the land.

But it is not enough to achieve these purposes alone. It is not enough to clothe and feed the body of this nation, to instruct, and inform its mind. For there is also the spirit. And of the three, the greatest is the spirit.

Without the body and the mind, as all men know, the nation could not live.

But if the spirit of America were killed, even though the nation's body and mind, constricted in an alien world, lived on, the America we know would have perished.

That spirit—that faith—speaks to us in our daily lives in ways often unnoticed, because they seem so obvious. It speaks to us here in the capital of the nation. It speaks to us through the processes of governing in the sovereignties of forty-eight states. It speaks to us in our counties, in our cities, in our towns, and in our villages. It speaks to us from the other nations of the hemisphere, and from those across the seas—the enslaved, as well as the free. Sometimes we fail to hear or heed these voices of freedom because to us the privilege of our freedom is such an old, old story.

The destiny of America was proclaimed in words of prophecy spoken by our first president in his first Inaugural in 1789—words almost directed, it would seem, to this year of 1941: "The preservation of the sacred fire of liberty and the destiny of the republican model of government are justly considered . . . deeply . . . finally, staked on the experiment intrusted to the hands of the American people."

If you and I in this later day lose that sacred fire—if we let it be smothered with doubt and fear—then we shall reject the destiny which Washington strove so valiantly and so triumphantly to establish. The preservation of the spirit and faith of the nation does, and will, furnish the highest justification for every sacrifice that we may make in the cause of national defense.

In the face of great perils never before encountered, our strong purpose is to protect and to perpetuate the integrity of democracy.

For this we muster the spirit of America, and the faith of America.

We do not retreat. We are not content to stand still. As Americans, we go forward, in the service of our country, by the will of God.

33.

A Nation Must Believe in Three Things

Speech Dedicating His Presidential Library
Hyde Park, New York, June 30, 1941

Donating his books and papers to the nation, FDR created the first Presidential Library. And clearly reflecting his commitment to the progressive development of American historical memory and imagination, he opened his remarks dedicating the library by speaking of the importance of remembering the past.

It seems to me that the dedication of a library is in itself an act of faith.

To bring together the records of the past and to house them in buildings where they will be preserved for the use of men and women in the future, a nation must believe in three things.

It must believe in the past.

It must believe in the future.

It must, above all, believe in the capacity of its own people so to learn from the past that they can gain in judgment in creating their own future.

Among democracies, I think through all the recorded history of the world, the building of permanent institutions like libraries and museums for the use of all the people flourishes. And that is especially true in our own land, because we believe that people ought to work out for themselves, and through their own study, the determination of their best interest rather than accept such so-called information as may be handed out to them by certain types of self-constituted leaders who decide what is best for them.

And so it is in keeping with the well-considered trend of these difficult days that we are distributing our own historical collections more widely than ever before throughout our land. From the point of view of the safety—the physical safety—of our records, it is wiser that they be not too greatly concentrated. From the point of view of accessibility, modern methods make dissemination practicable.

This particular Library is but one of many new libraries. And so, because it happens to be a national one, I as president have the privilege of accepting this newest house in which people's records are preserved—public papers and collections that refer to our own period of history.

And this latest addition to the archives of America is dedicated at a moment when government of the people by themselves is being attacked everywhere.

It is, therefore, proof—if any proof is needed—that our confidence in the future of democracy has not diminished in this nation and will not diminish.

34.

Yesterday, December 7, 1941—A Date Which Will Live in Infamy

Speech to a Joint Session of Congress
Washington, DC, December 8, 1941

On the day following the Japanese attack on Pearl Harbor in the Hawaiian Islands, Roosevelt went before Congress to request a Declaration of War. The Senate voted in favor 82–0, and the House of Representatives 388–1. A few days later, on December 11, Japan's Axis allies, Germany and Italy, declared war on the United States. Expressing the outrage of almost all Americans, FDR's "a date which will live in infamy" are perhaps his best remembered words.

Mr. Vice President, and Mr. Speaker, and members of the Senate and House of Representatives:

Yesterday, December 7, 1941—a date which will live in infamy—the United States of America was suddenly and deliberately attacked by naval and air forces of the Empire of Japan.

The United States was at peace with that nation and, at the solicitation of Japan, was still in conversation with its government and its emperor looking toward the maintenance of peace in the Pacific. Indeed, one hour after Japanese air squadrons had commenced bombing in the American Island of Oahu, the Japanese ambassador to the United States and his colleague delivered to our Secretary of State a formal reply to a recent American message. And while this reply stated that it seemed useless to continue the existing diplomatic negotiations, it contained no threat or hint of war or of armed attack.

It will be recorded that the distance of Hawaii from Japan makes it obvious that the attack was deliberately planned many days or even weeks ago. During the intervening time the Japanese government has deliberately sought to deceive the United States by false statements and expressions of hope for continued peace.

The attack yesterday on the Hawaiian Islands has caused severe damage to American naval and military forces. I regret to tell you that very many American lives have been lost. In addition American ships have been reported torpedoed on the high seas between San Francisco and Honolulu.

Yesterday the Japanese government also launched an attack against Malaya.

Last night Japanese forces attacked Hong Kong.

Last night Japanese forces attacked Guam.

Last night Japanese forces attacked the Philippine Islands.

Last night the Japanese attacked Wake Island. And this morning the Japanese attacked Midway Island.

Japan has, therefore, undertaken a surprise offensive extending throughout the Pacific area. The facts of yesterday and today speak for themselves. The people of the United States have already formed their opinions and well understand the implications to the very life and safety of our nation.

As Commander in Chief of the Army and Navy I have directed that all measures be taken for our defense.

But always will our whole nation remember the character of the onslaught against us.

No matter how long it may take us to overcome this premeditated invasion, the American people in their righteous might will win through to absolute victory.

I believe that I interpret the will of the Congress and of the people when I assert that we will not only defend ourselves to the uttermost but will make it very certain that this form of treachery shall never again endanger us.

Hostilities exist. There is no blinking at the fact that our people, our territory, and our interests are in grave danger.

With confidence in our armed forces—with the unbounding determination of our people—we will gain the inevitable triumph—so help us God.

I ask that the Congress declare that since the unprovoked and dastardly attack by Japan on Sunday, December 7, 1941, a state of war has existed between the United States and the Japanese Empire.

35.

No Date in the Long History of Freedom Means More

Radio Speech to the Nation
December 15, 1941

Early in 1941, New York City mayor—and the newly appointed first director of the Office of Civilian Defense—Fiorello La Guardia proposed to FDR that the United States celebrate the 150th anniversary of the Bill of Rights on December 15. Of course, nobody imagined that Bill of Rights Day would follow just one week after the nation was to enter the Second World War. Commemorative events took place around the country, culminating in the broadcast over all four radio networks of We Hold These Truths, *a play specially prepared for the occasion by the renowned radio producer and writer Norman Corwin that was performed by a cast of major Hollywood actors and followed by this address from the president.*

Free Americans:

No date in the long history of freedom means more to liberty-loving men in all liberty-loving countries than the fifteenth day of December, 1791. On that day, 150 years ago, a new nation, through an elected Congress, adopted a declaration of human rights which has influenced the thinking of all mankind from one end of the world to the other.

There is not a single Republic of this hemisphere which has not adopted in its fundamental law the basic principles of freedom of man and freedom of mind enacted in the American Bill of Rights.

There is not a country, large or small, on this continent and in this world which has not felt the influence of that document, directly or indirectly.

Indeed, prior to the year 1933, the essential validity of the American Bill of Rights was accepted everywhere at least in principle. Even today, with the exception of Germany, Italy, and Japan, the peoples of the whole world—in all probability four-fifths of them—support its principles, its teachings, and its glorious results.

But, in the year 1933, there came to power in Germany a political clique which did not accept the declarations of the American bill of human rights as valid: a small clique of ambitious and unscrupulous politicians whose announced and admitted platform was precisely the destruction of the rights that instrument declared. Indeed the entire program and goal of these political and moral tigers was nothing more than the overthrow, throughout the earth, of the great revolution of human liberty of which our American Bill of Rights is the mother charter.

The truths which were self-evident to Thomas Jefferson—which have been self-evident to the six generations of Americans who followed him— were to these men hateful. The rights to life, liberty, and the pursuit of happiness which seemed to the Founders of the Republic, and which seem to us, inalienable, were, to Hitler and his fellows, empty words which they proposed to cancel forever.

The propositions they advanced to take the place of Jefferson's inalienable rights were these:

That the individual human being has no rights whatsoever in himself and by virtue of his humanity;

That the individual human being has no right to a soul of his own, or a mind of his own, or a tongue of his own, or a trade of his own; or even to live where he pleases or to marry the woman he loves;

That his only duty is the duty of obedience, not to his God, not to his conscience, but to Adolf Hitler; and that his only value is his value, not as a man, but as a unit of the Nazi state.

To Hitler the ideal of the people, as we conceive it—the free, self-governing, and responsible people—is incomprehensible. The people, to Hitler, are "the masses" and the highest human idealism is, in his own words, that a man should wish to become "a dust particle" of the order "of force" which is to shape the universe.

To Hitler, the government, as we conceive it, is an impossible conception. The government to him is not the servant and the instrument of the people but their absolute master and the dictator of their every act.

To Hitler the church, as we conceive it, is a monstrosity to be destroyed by every means at his command. The Nazi church is to be the "National Church," a pagan church, "absolutely and exclusively in the service of but one doctrine, one race, one nation."

To Hitler, the freedom of men to think as they please and speak as they please and worship as they please is, of all things imaginable, most hateful and most desperately to be feared.

The issue of our time, the issue of the war in which we are engaged, is the issue forced upon the decent, self-respecting peoples of the earth by the aggressive dogmas of this attempted revival of barbarism; this proposed return to tyranny; this effort to impose again upon the peoples of the world doctrines of absolute obedience, of dictatorial rule, of the suppression of truth, of the oppression of conscience, which the free nations of the earth have long ago rejected.

What we face is nothing more nor less than an attempt to overthrow and to cancel out the great upsurge of human liberty of which the American Bill of Rights is the fundamental document: to force the peoples of the earth, and among them the peoples of this continent and this nation, to accept again the absolute authority and despotic rule from which the courage and the resolution and the sacrifices of their ancestors liberated them many, many years ago.

It is an attempt which could succeed only if those who have inherited the gift of liberty had lost the manhood to preserve it. But we Americans know that the determination of this generation of our people to preserve liberty is as fixed and certain as the determination of that early generation of Americans to win it.

We will not, under any threat, or in the face of any danger, surrender the guarantees of liberty our forefathers framed for us in our Bill of Rights.

We hold with all the passion of our hearts and minds to those commitments of the human spirit.

We are solemnly determined that no power or combination of powers of this earth shall shake our hold upon them.

We covenant with each other before all the world, that having taken up arms in the defense of liberty, we will not lay them down before liberty is once again secure in the world we live in. For that security we pray; for that security we act—now and evermore.

36.

Tyranny, Like Hell, Is Not Easily Conquered ...

Fireside Chat
February 23, 1942

In this Fireside Chat broadcast on Washington's birthday weekend, Roosevelt sought to calm American anxieties in the face of Japanese advances in the Pacific. The White House issued a call to Americans to secure a copy of a world map (the demand for which was so great that when stores sold out of them newspapers printed them as centerfolds). In a speech that the New York Times *called "one of the greatest of Roosevelt's career," the president not only explained to Americans the global character of the struggle in which they were now engaged, but also—recalling Thomas Paine's stirring words of his first American Crisis Paper, written during the darkest days of the American Revolution—reminded them once again of who they were and what they were capable of doing against the greatest of odds.*

My fellow Americans:

Washington's birthday is a most appropriate occasion for us to talk with each other about things as they are today and things as we know they shall be in the future.

For eight years, General Washington and his Continental Army were faced continually with formidable odds and recurring defeats. Supplies and equipment were lacking. In a sense, every winter was a Valley Forge. Throughout the thirteen states there existed fifth columnists—and selfish men, jealous men, fearful men, who proclaimed that Washington's cause was hopeless, and that he should ask for a negotiated peace.

Washington's conduct in those hard times has provided the model for all Americans ever since—a model of moral stamina. He held to his course, as it had been charted in the Declaration of Independence. He and the brave men who served with him knew that no man's life or fortune was secure, without freedom and free institutions.

The present great struggle has taught us increasingly that freedom of person and security of property anywhere in the world depend upon the security of the rights and obligations of liberty and justice everywhere in the world.

This war is a new kind of war. It is different from all other wars of the past, not only in its methods and weapons but also in its geography. It is warfare in terms of every continent, every island, every sea, every air lane in the world.

That is the reason why I have asked you to take out and spread before you a map of the whole earth, and to follow with me the references which I shall make to the world-encircling battle lines of this war. Many questions will, I fear, remain unanswered tonight; but I know you will realize that I cannot cover everything in any one short report to the people.

The broad oceans which have been heralded in the past as our protection from attack have become endless battlefields on which we are constantly being challenged by our enemies.

We must all understand and face the hard fact that our job now is to fight at distances which extend all the way around the globe.

We fight at these vast distances because that is where our enemies are. Until our flow of supplies gives us clear superiority we must keep on striking our enemies wherever and whenever we can meet them, even if, for a while, we have to yield ground. Actually, though, we are taking a heavy toll of the enemy every day that goes by.

We must fight at these vast distances to protect our supply lines and our lines of communication with our allies—protect these lines from the enemies who are bending every ounce of their strength, striving against time, to cut them. The object of the Nazis and the Japanese is to separate the United States, Britain, China, and Russia, and to isolate them one from another, so that each will be surrounded and cut off from sources of supplies and reinforcements. It is the old familiar Axis policy of "divide and conquer."

There are those who still think in terms of the days of sailing ships. They advise us to pull our warships and our planes and our merchant ships into our own home waters and concentrate solely on last-ditch defense. But let me illustrate what would happen if we followed such foolish advice.

Look at your map. Look at the vast area of China, with its millions of fighting men. Look at the vast area of Russia, with its powerful armies and proven military might. Look at the British Isles, Australia, New Zealand, the Dutch Indies, India, the Near East, and the continent of Africa, with their resources of raw materials, and of peoples determined to resist Axis domination. Look too at North America, Central America, and South America.

It is obvious what would happen if all of these great reservoirs of power were cut off from each other either by enemy action or by self-imposed isolation:

First, in such a case, we could no longer send aid of any kind to China—to the brave people who, for nearly five years, have withstood Japanese assault, destroyed hundreds of thousands of Japanese soldiers and vast quantities of Japanese war munitions. It is essential that we help China in her magnificent defense and in her inevitable counteroffensive—for that is one important element in the ultimate defeat of Japan.

Second, if we lost communication with the Southwest Pacific, all of that area, including Australia and New Zealand and the Dutch Indies, would fall under Japanese domination. Japan in such a case could release great numbers of ships and men to launch attacks on a large scale against the coasts of the Western Hemisphere—South America and Central America, and North America—including Alaska. At the same time, she could immediately extend her conquests in the other direction toward India, and through the Indian Ocean to Africa, to the Near East, and try to join forces with Germany and Italy.

Third, if we were to stop sending munitions to the British and the Russians in the Mediterranean, in the Persian Gulf, and the Red Sea, we would be helping the Nazis to overrun Turkey, Syria, Iraq, Persia, Egypt and the Suez Canal, the whole coast of North Africa itself, and with that inevitably the whole coast of West Africa—putting Germany within easy striking distance of South America—fifteen hundred miles away.

Fourth, if by such a fatuous policy we ceased to protect the North Atlantic supply line to Britain and to Russia, we would help to cripple the splendid counteroffensive by Russia against the Nazis, and we would help to deprive Britain of essential food supplies and munitions.

Those Americans who believed that we could live under the illusion of isolationism wanted the American eagle to imitate the tactics of the ostrich. Now, many of those same people, afraid that we may be sticking our necks out, want our national bird to be turned into a turtle. But we prefer to retain the eagle as it is—flying high and striking hard.

I know that I speak for the mass of the American people when I say that we reject the turtle policy and will continue increasingly the policy of carrying the war to the enemy in distant lands and distant waters—as far away as possible from our own home grounds.

There are four main lines of communication now being traveled by our ships: the North Atlantic, the South Atlantic, the Indian Ocean, and the South Pacific. These routes are not one-way streets—for the ships that carry our troops and munitions outbound bring back essential raw materials which we require for our own use.

The maintenance of these vital lines is a very tough job. It is a job which requires tremendous daring, tremendous resourcefulness, and, above all, tremendous production of planes and tanks and guns and also of the ships to carry them. And I speak again for the American people when I say that we can and will do that job.

The defense of the worldwide lines of communication demands relatively safe use by us of the sea and of the air along the various routes; and this, in turn, depends upon control by the United Nations of many strategic bases along those routes.

Control of the air involves the simultaneous use of two types of planes—first, the long-range heavy bomber; and second, light bombers, dive bombers, torpedo planes, and short-range pursuit planes, all of which are essential to the protection of the bases and of the bombers themselves.

Heavy bombers can fly under their own power from here to the Southwest Pacific; but the smaller planes cannot. Therefore, these lighter planes have to be packed in crates and sent on board cargo ships. Look at your map again; and you will see that the route is long—and at many places perilous—either across the South Atlantic all the way around South Africa and the Cape of Good Hope, or from California to the East Indies direct. A vessel can make a round trip by either route in about four months, or only three round trips in a whole year.

In spite of the length, and in spite of the difficulties of this transportation, I can tell you that in two and a half months we already have a large number of bombers and pursuit planes, manned by American pilots and crews, which are now in daily contact with the enemy in the Southwest Pacific. And thousands of American troops are today in that area engaged in operations not only in the air but on the ground as well.

In this battle area, Japan has had an obvious initial advantage. For she could fly even her short-range planes to the points of attack by using many stepping stones open to her—bases in a multitude of Pacific islands and also bases on the China coast, Indo-China coast, and in Thailand and Malay coasts. Japanese troop transports could go south from Japan and from China through the narrow China Sea which can be protected by Japanese planes throughout its whole length.

I ask you to look at your maps again, particularly at that portion of the Pacific Ocean lying west of Hawaii. Before this war even started, the Philippine Islands were already surrounded on three sides by Japanese power. On the west, the China side, the Japanese were in possession of the coast of China and the coast of Indo-China which had been yielded to them by the Vichy French. On the north are the islands of Japan themselves, reaching down almost to northern Luzon. On the east are the Mandated Islands—which Japan had occupied exclusively, and had fortified in absolute violation of her written word.

The islands that lie between Hawaii and the Philippines, these islands, hundreds of them, appear only as small dots on most maps. But they cover a large strategic area. Guam lies in the middle of them—a lone outpost which we have never fortified.

Under the Washington Treaty of 1921 we had solemnly agreed not to add to the fortification of the Philippines. We had no safe naval bases there, so we could not use the islands for extensive naval operations.

Immediately after this war started, the Japanese forces moved down on either side of the Philippines to numerous points south of them—thereby completely encircling the Philippines from north, south, east, and west.

It is that complete encirclement, with control of the air by Japanese land-based aircraft, which has prevented us from sending substantial reinforcements of men and material to the gallant defenders of the Philippines. For forty years it has always been our strategy—a strategy born of necessity—that in the event of a full-scale attack on the islands by Japan, we should fight a delaying action, attempting to retire slowly into Bataan Peninsula and Corregidor.

We knew that the war as a whole would have to be fought and won by a process of attrition against Japan itself. We knew all along that, with our greater resources, we could out-build Japan and ultimately overwhelm her on sea, on land, and in the air. We knew that, to attain our objective, many varieties of operations would be necessary in areas other than the Philippines.

Now nothing that has occurred in the past two months has caused us to revise this basic strategy of necessity—except that the defense put up by General MacArthur has magnificently exceeded the previous estimates of endurance; and he and his men are gaining eternal glory therefor.

MacArthur's army of Filipinos and Americans, and the forces of the United Nations in China, in Burma, and the Netherlands East Indies, are all together fulfilling the same essential task. They are making Japan pay an increasingly terrible price for her ambitious attempts to seize control of the whole Asiatic world. Every Japanese transport sunk off Java is one less transport that they can use to carry reinforcements to their army opposing General MacArthur in Luzon.

It has been said that Japanese gains in the Philippines were made possible only by the success of their surprise attack on Pearl Harbor. I tell you that this is not so.

Even if the attack had not been made your map will show that it would have been a hopeless operation for us to send the fleet to the Philippines through thousands of miles of ocean, while all those island bases were under the sole control of the Japanese.

The consequences of the attack on Pearl Harbor—serious as they were—have been wildly exaggerated in other ways. And these exaggerations come originally from Axis propagandists; but they have been repeated, I regret to say, by Americans in and out of public life.

You and I have the utmost contempt for Americans who, since Pearl Harbor, have whispered or announced "off the record" that there was no longer any Pacific Fleet—that the fleet was all sunk or destroyed on December 7—that more than a thousand of our planes were destroyed on the ground. They have suggested slyly that the government has withheld the truth about casualties—that eleven or twelve thousand men were killed at Pearl Harbor instead of the figures as officially announced. They have even served the enemy propagandists by spreading the incredible story that shiploads of bodies of our honored American dead were about to arrive in New York Harbor to be put into a common grave.

Almost every Axis broadcast—Berlin, Rome, Tokyo—directly quotes Americans who, by speech or in the press, make damnable misstatements such as these.

The American people realize that in many cases details of military operations cannot be disclosed until we are absolutely certain that the announcement will not give to the enemy military information which he does not already possess.

Your government has unmistakable confidence in your ability to hear the worst, without flinching or losing heart. You must, in turn, have complete confidence that your government is keeping nothing from you except information that will help the enemy in his attempt to destroy us. In a democracy there is always a solemn pact of truth between government and the people; but there must also always be a full use of discretion and that word "discretion" applies to the critics of government, as well.

This is war. The American people want to know, and will be told, the general trend of how the war is going. But they do not wish to help the enemy any more than our fighting forces do; and they will pay little attention to the rumor-mongers and the poison peddlers in our midst.

To pass from the realm of rumor and poison to the field of facts: The number of our officers and men killed in the attack on Pearl Harbor on December 7 was 2,340, and the number wounded was 946. Of all the combatant ships based at Pearl Harbor—battleships, heavy cruisers, light cruisers, aircraft carriers, destroyers, and submarines—only three are permanently put out of commission.

Very many of the ships of the Pacific Fleet were not even in Pearl Harbor. Some of those that were there were hit very slightly; and others that were damaged have either rejoined the fleet by now or are still undergoing repairs. And when those repairs are completed, the ships will be more efficient fighting machines than they were before.

The report that we lost more than a thousand planes at Pearl Harbor is as baseless as the other weird rumors. The Japanese do not know just how many planes they destroyed that day, and I am not going to tell them. But I can say that to date-—and including Pearl Harbor—we have destroyed considerably more Japanese planes than they have destroyed of ours.

We have most certainly suffered losses—from Hitler's U-boats in the Atlantic as well as from the Japanese in the Pacific—and we shall suffer more of them before the turn of the tide. But, speaking for the United States of America, let me say once and for all to the people of the world: We Americans have been compelled to yield ground, but we will regain it. We and the other United Nations are committed to the destruction of the militarism of Japan and Germany. We are daily increasing our strength. Soon, we and not our enemies will have the offensive; we, not they, will win the final battles; and we, not they, will make the final peace.

Conquered nations in Europe know what the yoke of the Nazis is like. And the people of Korea and of Manchuria know in their flesh the harsh despotism of Japan. All of the people of Asia know that if there is to be an honorable and decent future for any of them or any of us, that future depends on victory by the United Nations over the forces of Axis enslavement.

If a just and durable peace is to be attained, or even if all of us are merely to save our own skins, there is one thought for us here at home to keep uppermost—the fulfillment of our special task of production.

Germany, Italy, and Japan are very close to their maximum output of planes, guns, tanks, and ships. The United Nations are not—especially the United States of America.

Our first job then is to build up production—uninterrupted production—so that the United Nations can maintain control of the seas and attain control of the air—not merely a slight superiority, but an overwhelming superiority.

On January 6 of this year, I set certain definite goals of production for airplanes, tanks, guns, and ships. The Axis propagandists called them fantastic. Tonight, nearly two months later, and after a careful survey of progress by Donald Nelson and others charged with responsibility for our production, I can tell you that those goals will be attained.

In every part of the country, experts in production and the men and women at work in the plants are giving loyal service. With few exceptions, labor, capital, and farming realize that this is no time either to make undue profits or to gain special advantages, one over the other.

We are calling for new plants and additions to old plants. We are calling for plant conversion to war needs. We are seeking more men and more women to run them. We are working longer hours. We are coming to realize that one extra plane or extra tank or extra gun or extra ship completed tomorrow may, in a few months, turn the tide on some distant battlefield; it may make the difference between life and death for some of our own fighting men. We know now that if we lose this war it will be generations or even centuries before our conception of democracy can live again. And we can lose this war only if we slow up our effort or if we waste our ammunition sniping at each other.

Here are three high purposes for every American:

1. We shall not stop work for a single day. If any dispute arises we shall keep on working while the dispute is solved by mediation, conciliation, or arbitration—until the war is won.
2. We shall not demand special gains or special privileges or special advantages for any one group or occupation.
3. We shall give up conveniences and modify the routine of our lives if our country asks us to do so. We will do it cheerfully, remembering that the common enemy seeks to destroy every home and every freedom in every part of our land.

This generation of Americans has come to realize, with a present and personal realization, that there is something larger and more important than the life of any individual or of any individual group—something for which a man will sacrifice, and gladly sacrifice, not only his pleasures, not only his goods, not only his associations with those he loves, but his life itself. In time of crisis when the future is in the balance, we come to understand, with full recognition and devotion, what this nation is, and what we owe to it.

The Axis propagandists have tried in various evil ways to destroy our determination and our morale. Failing in that, they are now trying to destroy our confidence in our own allies. They say that the British are finished—that the Russians and the Chinese are about to quit. Patriotic and sensible Americans will reject these absurdities. And instead of listening to any of this crude propaganda, they will recall some of the things that Nazis and Japanese have said and are still saying about us.

Ever since this nation became the arsenal of democracy—ever since enactment of lend-lease—there has been one persistent theme through all Axis propaganda.

This theme has been that Americans are admittedly rich, that Americans have considerable industrial power—but that Americans are soft and decadent, that they cannot and will not unite and work and fight.

From Berlin, Rome, and Tokyo we have been described as a nation of weaklings—"playboys"—who would hire British soldiers, or Russian soldiers, or Chinese soldiers to do our fighting for us.

Let them repeat that now!

Let them tell that to General MacArthur and his men.

Let them tell that to the sailors who today are hitting hard in the far waters of the Pacific.

Let them tell that to the boys in the Flying Fortresses.

Let them tell that to the Marines!

The United Nations constitute an association of independent peoples of equal dignity and equal importance. The United Nations are dedicated to a common cause. We share equally and with equal zeal the anguish and the awful sacrifices of war. In the partnership of our common enterprise, we must share in a unified plan in which all of us must play our several parts, each of us being equally indispensable and dependent one on the other.

We have unified command and cooperation and comradeship.

We Americans will contribute unified production and unified acceptance of sacrifice and of effort. That means a national unity that can know no limitations of race or creed or selfish politics. The American people expect that much from themselves. And the American people will find ways and means of expressing their determination to their enemies, including the Japanese admiral who has said that he will dictate the terms of peace here in the White House.

We of the United Nations are agreed on certain broad principles in the kind of peace we seek. The Atlantic Charter applies not only to the parts of the world that border the Atlantic but to the whole world; disarmament of aggressors, self-determination of nations and peoples, and the four freedoms—freedom of speech, freedom of religion, freedom from want, and freedom from fear.

The British and the Russian people have known the full fury of Nazi onslaught. There have been times when the fate of London and Moscow was in serious doubt. But there was never the slightest question that either the British or the Russians would yield. And today all the United Nations salute the superb Russian Army as it celebrates the twenty-fourth anniversary of its first assembly.

Though their homeland was overrun, the Dutch people are still fighting stubbornly and powerfully overseas.

The great Chinese people have suffered grievous losses; Chungking has been almost wiped out of existence—yet it remains the capital of an unbeatable China.

That is the conquering spirit which prevails throughout the United Nations in this war.

The task that we Americans now face will test us to the uttermost. Never before have we been called upon for such a prodigious effort. Never before have we had so little time in which to do so much.

"These are the times that try men's souls." Tom Paine wrote those words on a drumhead, by the light of a campfire. That was when Washington's little army of ragged, rugged men was retreating across New Jersey, having tasted nothing but defeat.

And General Washington ordered that these great words written by Tom Paine be read to the men of every regiment in the Continental Army, and this was the assurance given to the first American armed forces:

"The summer soldier and the sunshine patriot will, in this crisis, shrink from the service of their country; but he that stands it now, deserves the love and thanks of man and woman. Tyranny, like hell, is not easily conquered; yet we have this consolation with us, that the harder the sacrifice, the more glorious the triumph."

So spoke Americans in the year 1776.

So speak Americans today!

37.

We Should Never Forget the Things We Are Fighting For

State of the Union Address
Washington, DC, January 7, 1943

The year 1942 proved to be, as FDR had said in his Washington's Birthday Fireside Chat, a time that "tried men's souls." But the struggle against Japan, Germany, and Italy was just beginning. In his 1943 State of the Union address (formerly known as the Annual Message to Congress), Roosevelt sought to remind Americans of what was at stake and to rally them to "redouble" their efforts on all fronts—that is, to go all out on both the military front overseas and the production front at home. As he stated it: "The issue of this war is the basic issue between those who believe in mankind and those who do not—the ancient issue between those who put their faith in the people and those who put their faith in dictators and tyrants."

Mr. Vice President, Mr. Speaker, members of the Seventy-eighth Congress:

This Seventy-eighth Congress assembles in one of the great moments in the history of the nation. The past year was perhaps the most crucial for modern civilization; the coming year will be filled with violent conflicts—yet with high promise of better things.

We must appraise the events of 1942 according to their relative importance; we must exercise a sense of proportion.

First in importance in the American scene has been the inspiring proof of the great qualities of our fighting men. They have demonstrated these qualities in adversity as well as in victory. As long as our flag flies over this Capitol, Americans will honor the soldiers, sailors, and marines who fought our first battles of this war against overwhelming odds the heroes, living and dead, of Wake and Bataan and Guadalcanal, of the Java Sea and Midway and the North Atlantic convoys. Their unconquerable spirit will live forever. . . .

I cannot prophesy. I cannot tell you when or where the United Nations are going to strike next in Europe. But we are going to strike—and strike hard. . . .

Hitler and Mussolini will understand now the enormity of their miscalculations—that the Nazis would always have the advantage of superior air power as they did when they bombed Warsaw, and Rotterdam, and London, and Coventry. That superiority has gone—forever.

Yes, the Nazis and the Fascists have asked for it—and they are going to get it.

Our forward progress in this war has depended upon our progress on the production front. . . .

I wonder, is there any person among us so simple as to believe that all this could have been done without creating some dislocations in our normal national life, some inconveniences, and even some hardships?

Who can have hoped to have done this without burdensome government regulations which are a nuisance to everyone—including those who have the thankless task of administering them?

We all know that there have been mistakes—mistakes due to the inevitable process of trial and error inherent in doing big things for the first time. We all know that there have been too many complicated forms and questionnaires. I know about that. I have had to fill some of them out myself. . . .

Of course, there have been disturbances and inconveniences—and even hardships. And there will be many, many more before we finally win. Yes, 1943 will not be an easy year for us on the home front. We shall feel in many ways in our daily lives the sharp pinch of total war.

Fortunately, there are only a few Americans who place appetite above patriotism. The overwhelming majority realize that the food we send abroad is for essential military purposes, for our own and Allied fighting forces, and for necessary help in areas that we occupy.

We Americans intend to do this great job together. In our common labors we must build and fortify the very foundation of national unity— confidence in one another. . . .

We should never forget the things we are fighting for. But, at this critical period of the war, we should confine ourselves to the larger objectives and not get bogged down in argument over methods and details. . . .

I have reason to know that our boys at the front are concerned with two broad aims beyond the winning of the war; and their thinking and their opinion coincide with what most Americans here back home are mulling over. They know, and we know, that it would be inconceivable—it would, indeed, be sacrilegious—if this nation and the world did not attain some real, lasting good out of all these efforts and sufferings and bloodshed and death.

The men in our armed forces want a lasting peace, and, equally, they want permanent employment for themselves, their families, and their neighbors when they are mustered out at the end of the war.

Two years ago I spoke in my Annual Message of four freedoms. The blessings of two of them—freedom of speech and freedom of religion—are an essential part of the very life of this nation; and we hope that these blessings will be granted to all men everywhere.

The people at home, and the people at the front, are wondering a little about the third freedom—freedom from want. To them it means that when they are mustered out, when war production is converted to the economy of peace, they will have the right to expect full employment—full employment for themselves and for all able-bodied men and women in America who want to work.

They expect the opportunity to work, to run their farms, their stores, to earn decent wages. They are eager to face the risks inherent in our system of free enterprise.

They do not want a postwar America which suffers from undernourishment or slums—or the dole. They want no get-rich-quick era of bogus "prosperity" which will end for them in selling apples on a street corner, as happened after the bursting of the boom in 1929.

When you talk with our young men and our young women, you will find they want to work for themselves and for their families; they consider that they have the right to work; and they know that after the last war their fathers did not gain that right.

When you talk with our young men and women, you will find that with the opportunity for employment they want assurance against the evils of all major economic hazards—assurance that will extend from the cradle to the grave. And this great government can and must provide this assurance.

I have been told that this is no time to speak of a better America after the war. I am told it is a grave error on my part.

I dissent.

And if the security of the individual citizen, or the family, should become a subject of national debate, the country knows where I stand.

I say this now to this Seventy-eighth Congress, because it is wholly possible that freedom from want—the right of employment, the right of assurance against life's hazards—will loom very large as a task of America during the coming two years.

I trust it will not be regarded as an issue—but rather as a task for all of us to study sympathetically, to work out with a constant regard for the attainment of the objective, with fairness to all and with injustice to none.

In this war of survival we must keep before our minds not only the evil things we fight against but the good things we are fighting for. We fight to retain a great past—and we fight to gain a greater future.

Let us remember, too, that economic safety for the America of the future is threatened unless a greater economic stability comes to the rest of the world. We cannot make America an island in either a military or an economic sense. Hitlerism, like any other form of crime or disease, can grow from the evil seeds of economic as well as military feudalism.

Victory in this war is the first and greatest goal before us. Victory in the peace is the next. That means striving toward the enlargement of the security of man here and throughout the world—and, finally, striving for the fourth freedom—freedom from fear.

It is of little account for any of us to talk of essential human needs, of attaining security, if we run the risk of another World War in ten or twenty or fifty years. That is just plain common sense. Wars grow in size, in death and destruction, and in the inevitability of engulfing all nations, in inverse ratio to the shrinking size of the world as a result of the conquest of the air. I shudder to think of what will happen to humanity, including ourselves, if this war ends in an inconclusive peace, and another war breaks out when the babies of today have grown to fighting age.

Every normal American prays that neither he nor his sons nor his grandsons will be compelled to go through this horror again.

Undoubtedly a few Americans, even now, think that this nation can end this war comfortably and then climb back into an American hole and pull the hole in after them.

But we have learned that we can never dig a hole so deep that it would be safe against predatory animals. We have also learned that if we do not pull the fangs of the predatory animals of this world, they will multiply and grow in strength—and they will be at our throats again once more in a short generation.

Most Americans realize more clearly than ever before that modern war equipment in the hands of aggressor nations can bring danger overnight to our own national existence or to that of any other nation—or island—or continent. . . .

After the first World War we tried to achieve a formula for permanent peace, based on a magnificent idealism. We failed. But, by our failure, we have learned that we cannot maintain peace at this stage of human development by good intentions alone.

Today the United Nations are the mightiest military coalition in all history. They represent an overwhelming majority of the population of the world. Bound together in solemn agreement that they themselves will not commit acts of aggression or conquest against any of their neighbors, the United Nations can and must remain united for the maintenance of peace by preventing any attempt to rearm in Germany, in Japan, in Italy, or in any other nation which seeks to violate the Tenth Commandment—"Thou shalt not covet" . . .

The issue of this war is the basic issue between those who believe in mankind and those who do not—the ancient issue between those who put their faith in the people and those who put their faith in dictators and tyrants. There have always been those who did not believe in the people, who attempted to block their forward movement across history, to force them back to servility and suffering and silence.

The people have now gathered their strength. They are moving forward in their might and power—and no force, no combination of forces, no trickery, deceit, or violence, can stop them now. They see before them the hope of the world—a decent, secure, peaceful life for men everywhere.

I do not prophesy when this war will end.

But I do believe that this year of 1943 will give to the United Nations a very substantial advance along the roads that lead to Berlin and Rome and Tokyo.

I tell you it is within the realm of possibility that this Seventy-eighth Congress may have the historic privilege of helping greatly to save the world from future fear.

Therefore, let us all have confidence, let us redouble our efforts.

A tremendous, costly, long-enduring task in peace as well as in war is still ahead of us.

But, as we face that continuing task, we may know that the state of this nation is good—the heart of this nation is sound—the spirit of this nation is strong—the faith of this nation is eternal.

38.

We, at Home, Owe a Special and Continuing Obligation to These Men and Women

Message to Congress
October 27, 1943

In this special message to Congress, Roosevelt called on the nation's representatives to consider the creation and funding of a major postwar program to pay for the further education of America's military veterans, both men and women, which could prepare them for productive civilian peacetime employment. Sixteen million Americans served in the military during the war (350,000 of them women)—400,000 would not return home, and 800,000 returned wounded or injured. The speech was part of FDR's campaign to create what became known as the "GI Bill of Rights." Twelve million veterans would partake of the Bill's benefits and proceed to rebuild not only their own lives, but also the nation at the same time.

To the Congress:

On November 13, 1942, on signing the bill calling for the induction by Selective Service of young men eighteen and nineteen years old, I appointed a committee of educators, under the auspices of the War and Navy Departments, to study the problem of education of our service men and women after the war. The objective was to enable those young people, whose education had been interrupted, to resume their schooling, and to provide an opportunity for the education and technical training of other young men and women of ability, after their discharge from the armed services.

This committee has sent me a preliminary report which I am herewith transmitting to the Congress for its consideration, and, I hope, for its early action.

We, at home, owe a special and continuing obligation to these men and women in the armed services.

During the war we have seen to it that they have received the best training and equipment, the best food, shelter, and medical attention, the best protection and care which planning, ingenuity, physical resources, and money could furnish in time of war. But after the war shall have been won, the best way that we can repay a portion of that debt is to see to it, by planning and by action now, that those men and women are demobilized into an economy which is sound and prosperous, with a minimum of unemployment and dislocation; and that, with the assistance of government, they are given the opportunity to find a job for which they are fitted and trained, in a field which offers some reasonable assurance of well-being and continuous employment.

For many, what they desire most in the way of employment will require special training and further education. As a part of a general program for the benefit of the members of our armed services, I believe that the nation is morally obligated to provide this training and education and the necessary financial assistance by which they can be secured. It is an obligation which should be recognized now; and legislation to that end should be enacted as soon as possible.

This is a good time not merely to be thinking about the subject, but actually to do something about it. Nothing will be more conducive to the maintenance of high morale in our troops than the knowledge that steps are being taken now to give them education and technical training when the fighting is over. . . .

Vocational and educational opportunities for veterans should be of the widest range. There will be those of limited education who now appreciate, perhaps for the first time, the importance of general education, and who would welcome a year in school or college. There will be those who desire to learn a remunerative trade or to fit themselves more adequately for specialized work in agriculture or commerce. There will be others who want professional courses to prepare them for their life's work.

Lack of money should not prevent any veteran of this war from equipping himself for the most useful employment for which his aptitudes and willingness qualify him. The money invested in this training and schooling program will reap rich dividends in higher productivity, more intelligent leadership, and greater human happiness.

We must replenish our supply of persons qualified to discharge the heavy responsibilities of the postwar world. We have taught our youth how to wage war; we must also teach them how to live useful and happy lives in freedom, justice, and decency.

Specifically, I agree with the recommendations made by the committee in this regard as follows:

1. The federal government should make it financially feasible for every man and woman who has served honorably for a minimum period in the armed forces since September 16, 1940, to spend a period up to one calendar year in a school, a college, a technical institution, or in actual training in industry, so that he can further his education, learn a trade, or acquire the necessary knowledge and skill for farming, commerce, manufacturing, or other pursuits.

2. In addition, the federal government should make it financially possible for a limited number of ex-service men and women, selected for their special aptitudes, to carry on their general, technical, or professional education for a further period of one, two, or three years.

This assistance from government should include not only cost of instruction but a certain amount of money for maintenance.

One incidental benefit of permitting discharged veterans to put in a year or more of schooling or training would be to simplify and cushion the return to civilian employment of service personnel. And I might call to your attention the fact that it costs less per year to keep a man at school or college or training on the job, than to maintain him on active military duty for a year.

While the federal government should provide the necessary funds and should have the responsibility of seeing that they are spent providently and under generally accepted standards, the control of the educational processes and the certification of trainees and students should reside in the states and localities.

I am sure that the Congress will agree with me that the report of this committee constitutes a helpful and constructive point of departure in the working out of a practical program for the meeting of this situation. Various recommendations are contained in the report concerning the administration of the plan. While there may be differences as to some of the details, I am confident that the Congress will find merit in the general objectives.

So far as disabled soldiers are concerned, the Congress is aware that, pursuant to existing statutes, the Veterans Administration is prepared to conduct a program of rehabilitation for veterans with service-connected disability. The program is designed to provide for the special needs of war-disabled veterans, and to furnish educational and training opportunities to help them take their places in civilian life. The program has already been initiated, and will be expanded as the war proceeds.

The new program of the Federal Security Agency will make provisions for veterans whose disabilities are not service-connected.

The Army and the Navy require a large number of workers skilled and experienced in various occupations and professions. Men who are filling these posts are acquiring valuable training and experience. A man who has become a mechanical draftsman, a cartographer, a meteorologist, a cook, or a baker may succeed in finding a similar post in civilian life. In a great many other occupations, such as those dealing with tank or tractor maintenance and repair, or with radio operation and maintenance, men are acquiring basic skill and experience which will provide a solid foundation for learning a related civilian occupation.

In addition, the United States Armed Forces Institute, which is a joint operation of the Army and Navy, offers men and women in the armed services a chance to enroll in courses usually offered by colleges, high schools, technical and occupational schools, in which they can study in their off-duty time. The Institute prepares self-teaching textbooks which enable them to learn a subject entirely on their own initiative; or, if they prefer, they may join any one of hundreds of classes which have been or are being established in Army camps and posts and in Navy installations, and in Army and Navy hospitals, here in the United States and in places all over the world. Or if they wish, they can study by the correspondence method with the Institute or with one of its overseas branches the same as any student in a correspondence school.

Opportunities for vocational training and for systematic schooling within the armed services will be expanded and reoriented during periods of demobilization and up to the moment of discharge.

Therefore, if the Congress adopts the general objective outlined herein, our men and women in the armed forces will be afforded opportunities for continuance of their education and vocational training—first, during the war; second, during the demobilization period; and third, for a year or more after their separation from the service.

While the successful conclusion of this great war is by no means within our sight, yet it may well be said that the time to prepare for peace is at the height of war.

39.

We Have Accepted, So to Speak, a Second Bill of Rights

State of the Union Address
Washington, DC, January 11, 1944

With the tide of war definitely moving in favor of the United States and its "United Nations" allies, Roosevelt returned in his 1944 State of the Union address to his idea of creating a Declaration of Economic Rights (1932) and securing the Four Freedoms (1941). After urging Americans to continue to give their all to the war effort—and strongly warning them against those who might place greed above patriotism—he stated: "We have accepted, so to speak, a second Bill of Rights under which a new basis of security and prosperity can be established for all regardless of station, race, or creed." And he proceeded to propose nothing less than an "Economic Bill of Rights" for all Americans. He did so, confident that most Americans would support the idea, for surveys commissioned by the White House had indicated that the great majority of Americans definitely wanted to establish national health care, greater educational opportunities, and an expanded Social Security program. He also knew, however, that as much as Americans might support his call, the conservative coalition in Congress and powerful corporate business interests would vehemently oppose it. Nevertheless, he hoped Americans might one day secure such a bill of rights.

To the Congress:

This nation in the past two years has become an active partner in the world's greatest war against human slavery.

We have joined with like-minded people in order to defend ourselves in a world that has been gravely threatened with gangster rule.

But I do not think that any of us Americans can be content with mere survival. Sacrifices that we and our allies are making impose upon us all a sacred obligation to see to it that out of this war we and our children will gain something better than mere survival.

We are united in determination that this war shall not be followed by another interim which leads to new disaster—that we shall not repeat the tragic errors of ostrich isolationism—that we shall not repeat the excesses of the wild twenties when this nation went for a joy ride on a roller coaster which ended in a tragic crash. . . .

The overwhelming majority of our people have met the demands of this war with magnificent courage and understanding. They have accepted inconveniences; they have accepted hardships; they have accepted tragic sacrifices. And they are ready and eager to make whatever further contributions are needed to win the war as quickly as possible—if only they are given the chance to know what is required of them.

However, while the majority goes on about its great work without complaint, a noisy minority maintains an uproar of demands for special favors for special groups. There are pests who swarm through the lobbies of the Congress and the cocktail bars of Washington, representing these special groups as opposed to the basic interests of the nation as a whole. They have come to look upon the war primarily as a chance to make profits for themselves at the expense of their neighbors—profits in money or in terms of political or social preferment.

Such selfish agitation can be highly dangerous in wartime. It creates confusion. It damages morale. It hampers our national effort. It muddies the waters and therefore prolongs the war. . . .

If ever there was a time to subordinate individual or group selfishness to the national good, that time is now. . . .

Those who are doing most of the complaining are not deliberately striving to sabotage the national war effort. They are laboring under the delusion that the time is past when we must make prodigious sacrifices—that the war is already won and we can begin to slacken off. But the dangerous folly of that point of view can be measured by the distance that separates our troops from their ultimate objectives in Berlin and Tokyo—and by the sum of all the perils that lie along the way.

Overconfidence and complacency are among our deadliest enemies. . . .

Therefore, in order to concentrate all our energies and resources on winning the war, and to maintain a fair and stable economy at home, I recommend that the Congress adopt:

1. A realistic tax law—which will tax all unreasonable profits, both individual and corporate, and reduce the ultimate cost of the war to our sons and daughters. . . .
2. A continuation of the law for the renegotiation of war contracts—which will prevent exorbitant profits and assure fair prices to the government. For two long years I have pleaded with the Congress to take undue profits out of war.
3. A cost of food law—which will enable the government (a) to place a reasonable floor under the prices the farmer may expect for his production; and (b) to place a ceiling on the prices a consumer will have to pay for the food he buys. . . .
4. Early reenactment of the stabilization statute of October 1942. This expires June 30, 1944, and if it is not extended well in advance, the country might just as well expect price chaos by summer.

   We cannot have stabilization by wishful thinking. We must take positive action to maintain the integrity of the American dollar.
5. A national service law—which, for the duration of the war, will prevent strikes, and, with certain appropriate exceptions, will make available for war production or for any other essential services every able-bodied adult in this nation.

These five measures together form a just and equitable whole. I would not recommend a national service law unless the other laws were passed to keep down the cost of living, to share equitably the burdens of taxation, to hold the stabilization line, and to prevent undue profits.

The federal government already has the basic power to draft capital and property of all kinds for war purposes on a basis of just compensation.

As you know, I have for three years hesitated to recommend a national service act. Today, however, I am convinced of its necessity. Although I believe that we and our allies can win the war without such a measure, I am certain that nothing less than total mobilization of all our resources of manpower and capital will guarantee an earlier victory, and reduce the toll of suffering and sorrow and blood.

I have received a joint recommendation for this law from the heads of the War Department, the Navy Department, and the Maritime Commission. These are the men who bear responsibility for the procurement of the necessary arms and equipment, and for the successful prosecution of the war in the field. They say:

"When the very life of the nation is in peril the responsibility for service is common to all men and women. In such a time there can be no discrimination between the men and women who are assigned by the government to its defense at the battlefront and the men and women assigned to producing the vital materials essential to successful military operations. A prompt enactment of a National Service Law would be merely an expression of the universality of this responsibility."

I believe the country will agree that those statements are the solemn truth.

National service is the most democratic way to wage a war. Like selective service for the armed forces, it rests on the obligation of each citizen to serve his nation to his utmost where he is best qualified.

It does not mean reduction in wages. It does not mean loss of retirement and seniority rights and benefits. It does not mean that any substantial numbers of war workers will be disturbed in their present jobs. Let these facts be wholly clear. . . .

There are millions of American men and women who are not in this war at all. It is not because they do not want to be in it. But they want to know where they can best do their share. National service provides that direction. It will be a means by which every man and woman can find that inner satisfaction which comes from making the fullest possible contribution to victory.

I know that all civilian war workers will be glad to be able to say many years hence to their grandchildren: "Yes, I, too, was in service in the great war. I was on duty in an airplane factory, and I helped make hundreds of fighting planes. The government told me that in doing that I was performing my most useful work in the service of my country."

It is argued that we have passed the stage in the war where national service is necessary. But our soldiers and sailors know that this is not true. We are going forward on a long, rough road—and, in all journeys, the last miles are the hardest. And it is for that final effort—for the total defeat of our enemies—that we must mobilize our total resources. The national war program calls for the employment of more people in 1944 than in 1943. . . .

Our armed forces are valiantly fulfilling their responsibilities to our country and our people. Now the Congress faces the responsibility for taking those measures which are essential to national security in this the most decisive phase of the nation's greatest war.

Several alleged reasons have prevented the enactment of legislation which would preserve for our soldiers and sailors and marines the fundamental prerogative of citizenship—the right to vote. No amount of legalistic argument can becloud this issue in the eyes of these ten million American citizens. Surely the signers of the Constitution did not intend a document which, even in wartime, would be construed to take away the franchise of any of those who are fighting to preserve the Constitution itself.

Our soldiers and sailors and marines know that the overwhelming majority of them will be deprived of the opportunity to vote, if the voting machinery is left exclusively to the states under existing state laws—and that there is no likelihood of these laws being changed in time to enable them to vote at the next election. The Army and Navy have reported that it will be impossible effectively to administer forty-eight different soldier voting laws. It is the duty of the Congress to remove this unjustifiable discrimination against the men and women in our armed forces—and to do it as quickly as possible.

It is our duty now to begin to lay the plans and determine the strategy for the winning of a lasting peace and the establishment of an American standard of living higher than ever before known. We cannot be content, no matter how high that general standard of living may be, if some fraction of our people—whether it be one-third or one-fifth or one-tenth—is ill-fed, ill-clothed, ill-housed, and insecure.

This Republic had its beginning, and grew to its present strength, under the protection of certain inalienable political rights—among them the right of free speech, free press, free worship, trial by jury, freedom from unreasonable searches and seizures. They were our rights to life and liberty.

As our nation has grown in size and stature, however—as our industrial economy expanded—these political rights proved inadequate to assure us equality in the pursuit of happiness.

We have come to a clear realization of the fact that true individual freedom cannot exist without economic security and independence. "Necessitous men are not free men." People who are hungry and out of a job are the stuff of which dictatorships are made.

In our day these economic truths have become accepted as self-evident. We have accepted, so to speak, a second Bill of Rights under which a new basis of security and prosperity can be established for all regardless of station, race, or creed.

Among these are:

The right to a useful and remunerative job in the industries or shops or farms or mines of the nation;

The right to earn enough to provide adequate food and clothing and recreation;

The right of every farmer to raise and sell his products at a return which will give him and his family a decent living;

The right of every businessman, large and small, to trade in an atmosphere of freedom from unfair competition and domination by monopolies at home or abroad;

The right of every family to a decent home;

The right to adequate medical care and the opportunity to achieve and enjoy good health;

The right to adequate protection from the economic fears of old age, sickness, accident, and unemployment;

The right to a good education.

All of these rights spell security. And after this war is won we must be prepared to move forward, in the implementation of these rights, to new goals of human happiness and well-being.

America's own rightful place in the world depends in large part upon how fully these and similar rights have been carried into practice for our citizens. For unless there is security here at home there cannot be lasting peace in the world.

One of the great American industrialists of our day—a man who has rendered yeoman service to his country in this crisis—recently emphasized the grave dangers of "rightist reaction" in this nation. All clear-thinking businessmen share his concern. Indeed, if such reaction should develop— if history were to repeat itself and we were to return to the so-called "normalcy" of the 1920s—then it is certain that even though we shall have conquered our enemies on the battlefields abroad, we shall have yielded to the spirit of Fascism here at home.

I ask the Congress to explore the means for implementing this Economic Bill of Rights—for it is definitely the responsibility of the Congress so to do. Many of these problems are already before committees of the Congress in the form of proposed legislation. I shall from time to time communicate with the Congress with respect to these and further proposals. In the event that no adequate program of progress is evolved, I am certain that the nation will be conscious of the fact.

Our fighting men abroad—and their families at home—expect such a program and have the right to insist upon it. It is to their demands that this government should pay heed rather than to the whining demands of selfish pressure groups who seek to feather their nests while young Americans are dying.

The foreign policy that we have been following—the policy that guided us at Moscow, Cairo, and Teheran—is based on the commonsense principle which was best expressed by Benjamin Franklin on July 4, 1776: "We must all hang together, or assuredly we shall all hang separately."

I have often said that there are no two fronts for America in this war. There is only one front. There is one line of unity which extends from the hearts of the people at home to the men of our attacking forces in our farthest outposts. When we speak of our total effort, we speak of the factory and the field, and the mine as well as of the battleground—we speak of the soldier and the civilian, the citizen and his government.

Each and every one of us has a solemn obligation under God to serve this nation in its most critical hour—to keep this nation great—to make this nation greater in a better world.

40.

The Right to Vote Must Be Open to Our Citizens Irrespective of Race, Color, or Creed

Radio Address from the White House
October 5, 1944

Running for a fourth term as president, FDR recognized the importance of winning the growing African American vote in the cities of the north. Northern blacks historically had voted for the "Party of Lincoln," but in the course of the early New Deal years most had come to see his presidency as the means by which they might more effectively confront both northern racial discrimination and southern racial segregation. In light of the ongoing struggle against Nazism/fascism and racism overseas, the massive participation of African Americans in the war effort, and concerted pressure by the growing civil rights movement, Roosevelt placed the question of voting rights directly on the political agenda in this national radio address.

My fellow Americans:

I am speaking to you tonight from the White House. I am speaking particularly on behalf of those Americans who, regardless of party—I hope you will remember that—very much hope that there will be recorded a large registration and a large vote this fall. I know, and many of you do, from personal experience how effective precinct workers of all parties throughout the nation can be in assuring a large vote.

We are holding a national election despite all the prophecies of some politicians and a few newspapers who have stated, time and again in the past, that it was my horrid and sinister purpose to abolish all elections and to deprive the American people of the right to vote.

These same people, caring more for material riches than human rights, try to build up bogies of dictatorship in this Republic, although they know that free elections will always protect our nation against any such possibility.

Nobody will ever deprive the American people of the right to vote except the American people themselves—and the only way they could do that is by not voting at all.

The continuing health and vigor of our democratic system depends on the public spirit and devotion of its citizens which find expression in the ballot box.

Every man and every woman in this nation—regardless of party—who has the right to register and to vote, and the opportunity to register and to vote, has also the sacred obligation to register and to vote. For the free and secret ballot is the real keystone of our American Constitutional system.

The American government has survived and prospered for more than a century and a half, and it is now at the highest peak of its vitality. This is primarily because when the American people want a change of government—even when they merely want "new faces"—they can raise the old electioneering battle cry of "throw the rascals out."

It is true that there are many undemocratic defects in voting laws in the various states, almost forty-eight different kinds of defects, and some of these produce injustices which prevent a full and free expression of public opinion.

The right to vote must be open to our citizens—irrespective of race, color, or creed—without tax or artificial restriction of any kind. The sooner we get to that basis of political equality, the better it will be for the country as a whole . . .

This year, for many millions of our young men in the armed forces and the merchant marine and similar services, it will be difficult in many cases—and impossible in some cases—to register and vote.

I think the people will be able to fix the responsibility for this state of affairs, for they know that during this past year there were politicians and others who quite openly worked to restrict the use of the ballot in this election, hoping selfishly for a small vote.

It is, therefore, all the more important that we here at home must not be slackers on registration day or on election day.

I wish to make a special appeal to the women of the nation to exercise their right to vote. Women have taken an active part in this war in many ways—in uniform, in plants and ship yards, in offices and stores and hospitals, on farms, and on railroads and buses. They have become more than ever a very integral part of our national effort.

I know how difficult it is, especially for the many millions of women now employed, to get away to register and vote. Many of them have to manage their households as well as their jobs, and a grateful nation remembers that.

But all women, whether employed directly in war jobs or not—women of all parties, and those not enrolled in any party this year have a double obligation to express by their votes what I know to be their keen interest in the affairs of government their obligation to themselves as citizens, and their obligation to their fighting husbands, and sons, and brothers, and sweethearts.

It may sound to you repetitious on my part, but it is my plain duty to reiterate to you that this war for the preservation of our civilization is not won yet. . . .

The power of the will of the American people expressed through the free ballot that I have been talking about is the surest protection against the weakening of our democracy by "regimentation" or by any alien doctrines.

And likewise it is a source of regret to all decent Americans that some political propagandists are now dragging red herrings across the trail of this national election.

For example, labor-baiters, bigots, and some politicians use the term "Communism" loosely, and apply it to every progressive social measure and to the views of every foreign-born citizen with whom they disagree. . . .

I have never sought, and I do not welcome the support of any person or group committed to Communism, or Fascism, or any other foreign ideology which would undermine the American system of government, or the American system of free competitive enterprise and private property.

That does not in the least interfere with the firm and friendly relationship which this nation has in this war, and will, I hope, continue to have with the people of the Soviet Union. The kind of economy that suits the Russian people, I take it is their own affair. The American people are glad and proud to be allied with the gallant people of Russia, not only in winning this war but in laying the foundations for the world peace which I hope will follow this war—and in keeping that peace.

We have seen our civilization in deadly peril. Successfully we have met the challenge, due to the steadfastness of our allies, to the aid we were able to give to our allies, and to the unprecedented outpouring of American manpower, American productivity, and American ingenuity—and to the magnificent courage and enterprise of our fighting men and our military leadership.

What is now being won in battle must not be lost by lack of vision, or lack of knowledge, or by lack of faith, or by division among ourselves and our allies.

We must, and I hope we will, continue to be united with our allies in a powerful world organization which is ready and able to keep the peace—if necessary by force.

To provide that assurance of international security is the policy, the effort, and the obligation of this administration.

We owe it to our posterity, we owe it to our heritage of freedom, we owe it to our God, to devote the rest of our lives and all of our capabilities to the building of a solid, durable structure of world peace.

41.

We Are Not Going to Turn the Clock Back!

Campaign Address
Chicago, Illinois, October 28, 1944

In this campaign speech at Soldiers Field in Chicago, Roosevelt reiterated his call for the creation of an Economic Bill of Rights. But it was not only the president who continued to advance the call. Both major labor federations— the Congress of Industrial Organizations (CIO) and the American Federation of Labor (AFL), which would merge in 1955 to become the AFL-CIO—ardently supported FDR's vision and worked hard to support his reelection bid. He would indeed win a fourth term as president.

The American people are now engaged in the greatest war of all history— and we are also engaged in a political campaign.

We are fighting this war and we are holding this election both for the same essential reason: because we have faith in democracy.

And there is no force and there is no combination of forces powerful enough to shake that faith.

As you know, I have had some experience in war—and I have also had a certain amount of previous experience in political campaigning. . . .

Tonight I want to talk simply to you about the future of America— about this land of ours, this land of unlimited opportunity. I shall give the Republican campaign orators some more opportunities to say—"me too."

Today, everything we do is devoted to the most important job before us—winning the war and bringing our men and women home as quickly as possible.

We have astonished the whole world and confounded our enemies with our stupendous war production, with the overwhelming courage and skill of our fighting men—with the bridge of ships carrying our munitions and men through the seven seas—with our gigantic fleet which has pounded the enemy all over the Pacific and has just driven through for another touchdown.

Yes, the American people are prepared to meet the problems of peace in the same bold way that they have met the problems of war.

For the American people are resolved that when our men and women return home from this war, they shall come back to the best possible place on the face of the earth—they shall come back to a place where all persons, regardless of race, and color, or creed, or place of birth, can live in peace and honor and human dignity—free to speak, free to pray as they wish—free from want—and free from fear.

Last January, in my message to the Congress on the State of the Union, I outlined an Economic Bill of Rights on which "a new basis of security and prosperity can be established for all."

And I repeat it now:

"The right of a useful and remunerative job in the industries or shops or farms or mines of the nation;

"The right to earn enough to provide adequate food and clothing and recreation;

"The right of every farmer to raise and sell his products at a return which will give him and his family a decent living;

"The right of every businessman, large and small, to trade in an atmosphere of freedom from unfair competition and domination by monopolies at home or abroad;

"The right of every family to a decent home;

"The right to adequate medical care and the opportunity to achieve and enjoy good health;

"The right to adequate protection from the economic fears of old age, sickness, accident, and unemployment;

"The right to a good education."

Now, what do those rights mean? They "spell security. And after this war is won we must be prepared to move forward, in the implementation of these rights, to new goals of human happiness and well-being."

Some people—I need not name them—have sneered at these ideals as well as at the ideals of the Atlantic Charter, the ideals of the Four Freedoms. They have said that they were the dreams of starry-eyed New Dealers—that it is silly to talk of them because we cannot attain these ideals tomorrow or the next day.

The American people have greater faith than that. I know that they agree with these objectives—that they demand them—that they are determined to get them—and that they are going to get them.

The American people have a good habit—the habit of going right ahead and accomplishing the impossible.

We know that, and other people know it. . . .

Now, this Economic Bill of Rights is the recognition of the simple fact that, in America, the future of the worker, the future of the farmer lies in the well-being of private enterprise; and that the future of private enterprise lies in the well-being of the worker and the farmer. It goes both ways.

And the well-being of the nation as a whole is synonymous with the well-being of each and every one of its citizens.

Now I have the possibly old-fashioned theory that when you have problems to solve, when you have objectives to achieve, you cannot get very far by just talking about them.

We have got to go out and do something!

To assure the full realization of the right to a useful and remunerative employment, an adequate program must, and if I have anything to do about it will, provide America with close to sixty million productive jobs.

I foresee an expansion of our peacetime productive capacity that will require new facilities, new plants, new equipment—capable of hiring millions of men.

I propose that the government do its part in helping private enterprise to finance expansion of our private industrial plant through normal investment channels.

For example, business, large and small, must be encouraged by the government to expand its plants, to replace its obsolete or worn-out equipment with new equipment. And to that end, the rate of depreciation on these new plants and facilities for tax purposes should be accelerated. That means more jobs for the worker, increased profits for the businessman, and a lower cost to the consumer.

In 1933, when my administration took office, vast numbers of our industrial workers were unemployed, our plants and our businesses were idle, our monetary and banking system was in ruins—our economic resources were running to waste.

But by 1940—before Pearl Harbor—we had increased our employment by ten million workers. We had converted a corporate loss of five and one-half billion dollars in 1932 to a corporate profit (after taxes) of nearly five billion dollars in 1940.

Obviously, to increase jobs after this war, we shall have to increase demand for our industrial and agricultural production not only here at home, but abroad also.

I am sure that every man and woman in this vast gathering here tonight will agree with me in my conviction that never again must we in the United States attempt to isolate ourselves from the rest of humanity.

I am convinced that, with congressional approval, the foreign trade of the United States can be trebled after the war—providing millions of more jobs.

Such cooperative measures provide the soundest economic foundation for a lasting peace. And, after this war, we do not intend to settle for anything less than a lasting peace.

When we think of the America of tomorrow, we think of many things.

One of them is the American home—in our cities, in our villages, on our farms. Millions of our people have never had homes worthy of American standards—well-built homes, with electricity and plumbing, air and sunlight.

The demand for homes and our capacity to build them call for a program of well over a million homes a year for at least ten years. Private industry can build and finance the vast majority of these homes. Government can and will assist and encourage private industry to do this, as it has for many years. For those very low income groups that cannot possibly afford decent homes, the federal government should continue to assist local housing authorities in meeting that need.

In the future America that we are talking about, we think of new highways, new parkways. We think of thousands of new airports to service the new commercial and private air travel which is bound to come after the war. We think of new planes, large and small, new cheap automobiles with low maintenance and operation costs. We think of new hospitals and new health clinics. We think of a new merchant marine for our expanded world trade.

My friends, think of these vast possibilities for industrial expansion— and you will foresee opportunities for more millions of jobs.

And with all that, our Economic Bill of Rights—like the sacred Bill of Rights of our Constitution itself—must be applied to all our citizens, irrespective of race, or creed, or color. . . .

The future of America, like its past, must be made by deeds—not words.

America has always been a land of action—a land of adventurous pioneering—a land of growing and building.

America must always be such a land.

The creed of our democracy is that liberty is acquired, liberty is kept by men and women who are strong, self-reliant, and possessed of such wisdom as God gives to mankind—men and women who are just, men and women who are understanding, and generous to others—men and women who are capable of disciplining themselves.

For they are the rulers, and they must rule themselves.

I believe in our democratic faith. I believe in the future of our country which has given eternal strength and vitality to that faith.

Here in Chicago you know a lot about that vitality.

And as I say good night to you, I say it in a spirit of faith—a spirit of hope—a spirit of confidence.

We are not going to turn the clock back!

We are going forward, my friends—forward with the fighting millions of our fellow countrymen.

We are going forward together.

42.

We Have Learned to Be Citizens of the World

Fourth Inaugural Address
Washington, DC, January 20, 1945

In his fourth inaugural address, Roosevelt sought not merely to warn Americans not to return to their isolationist ways of the past, but also to encourage them to take the lead in creating a United Nations Organization. He had run for vice president on the 1920 Democratic ticket. Critical to that campaign was the issue of American membership in the League of Nations. The Republicans opposed it; the Democrats favored it; the former won, and the United States stayed out of the League. But FDR had never abandoned the idea of assuring peace by establishing organized international cooperation to secure it.

Mr. Chief Justice, Mr. Vice President, my friends:

You will understand and, I believe, agree with my wish that the form of this inauguration be simple and its words brief.

We Americans of today, together with our allies, are passing through a period of supreme test. It is a test of our courage—of our resolve—of our wisdom—of our essential democracy.

If we meet that test—successfully and honorably—we shall perform a service of historic importance which men and women and children will honor throughout all time.

As I stand here today, having taken the solemn oath of office in the presence of my fellow countrymen—in the presence of our God—I know that it is America's purpose that we shall not fail.

In the days and the years that are to come, we shall work for a just and honorable peace, a durable peace, as today we work and fight for total victory in war.

We can and we will achieve such a peace.

We shall strive for perfection. We shall not achieve it immediately—but we still shall strive. We may make mistakes—but they must never be mistakes which result from faintness of heart or abandonment of moral principle.

I remember that my old schoolmaster, Dr. Peabody, said—in days that seemed to us then to be secure and untroubled: "Things in life will not always run smoothly. Sometimes we will be rising toward the heights—then all will seem to reverse itself and start downward. The great fact to remember is that the trend of civilization itself is forever upward; that a line drawn through the middle of the peaks and the valleys of the centuries always has an upward trend."

Our Constitution of 1787 was not a perfect instrument; it is not perfect yet. But it provided a firm base upon which all manner of men, of all races and colors and creeds, could build our solid structure of democracy.

Today, in this year of war, 1945, we have learned lessons—at a fearful cost—and we shall profit by them.

We have learned that we cannot live alone, at peace; that our own well-being is dependent on the well-being of other nations, far away. We have learned that we must live as men and not as ostriches, nor as dogs in the manger.

We have learned to be citizens of the world, members of the human community.

We have learned the simple truth, as Emerson said, that "The only way to have a friend is to be one."

We can gain no lasting peace if we approach it with suspicion and mistrust—or with fear. We can gain it only if we proceed with the understanding and the confidence and the courage which flow from conviction.

The Almighty God has blessed our land in many ways. He has given our people stout hearts and strong arms with which to strike mighty blows for freedom and truth. He has given to our country a faith which has become the hope of all peoples in an anguished world.

So we pray to Him now for the vision to see our way clearly to see the way that leads to a better life for ourselves and for all our fellow men—and to the achievement of His will to peace on earth.

43.

Let Us Move Forward with Strong and Active Faith

April 1945

Roosevelt passed away on April 12, 1945 in Warms Springs, Georgia, where in the 1920s he had established a rehabilitation center for polio sufferers. The following undelivered speech was to have been delivered as a Jefferson Day radio address on April 13, 1945.

Americans are gathered together this evening in communities all over the country to pay tribute to the living memory of Thomas Jefferson—one of the greatest of all democrats; and I want to make it clear that I am spelling that word "democrats" with a small *d*.

I wish I had the power, just for this evening, to be present at all of these gatherings.

In this historic year, more than ever before, we do well to consider the character of Thomas Jefferson as an American citizen of the world.

As minister to France, then as our first secretary of state and as our third president, Jefferson was instrumental in the establishment of the United States as a vital factor in international affairs.

It was he who first sent our Navy into far-distant waters to defend our rights. And the promulgation of the Monroe Doctrine was the logical development of Jefferson's far-seeing foreign policy.

Today this nation which Jefferson helped so greatly to build is playing a tremendous part in the battle for the rights of man all over the world.

Today we are part of the vast Allied force—a force composed of flesh and blood and steel and spirit—which is today destroying the makers of war, the breeders of hatred, in Europe and in Asia.

In Jefferson's time our Navy consisted of only a handful of frigates headed by the gallant USS *Constitution*—Old Ironsides—but that tiny Navy taught nations across the Atlantic that piracy in the Mediterranean—acts of aggression against peaceful commerce and the enslavement of their crews—was one of those things which, among neighbors, simply was not done.

Today we have learned in the agony of war that great power involves great responsibility. Today we can no more escape the consequences of German and Japanese aggression than could we avoid the consequences of attacks by the Barbary Corsairs a century and a half before.

We, as Americans, do not choose to deny our responsibility.

Nor do we intend to abandon our determination that, within the lives of our children and our children's children, there will not be a third world war.

We seek peace—enduring peace. More than an end to war, we want an end to the beginnings of all wars—yes, an end to this brutal, inhuman, and thoroughly impractical method of settling the differences between governments.

The once powerful, malignant Nazi state is crumbling. The Japanese war lords are receiving, in their own homeland, the retribution for which they asked when they attacked Pearl Harbor.

But the mere conquest of our enemies is not enough.

We must go on to do all in our power to conquer the doubts and the fears, the ignorance and the greed, which made this horror possible.

Thomas Jefferson, himself a distinguished scientist, once spoke of "the brotherly spirit of Science, which unites into one family all its votaries of whatever grade, and however widely dispersed throughout the different quarters of the globe."

Today, science has brought all the different quarters of the globe so close together that it is impossible to isolate them one from another.

Today we are faced with the preeminent fact that, if civilization is to survive, we must cultivate the science of human relationships—the ability of all peoples, of all kinds, to live together and work together, in the same world, at peace.

Let me assure you that my hand is the steadier for the work that is to be done, that I move more firmly into the task, knowing that you—millions and millions of you—are joined with me in the resolve to make this work endure.

The work, my friends, is peace. More than an end of this war—an end to the beginnings of all wars. Yes, an end, forever, to this impractical, unrealistic settlement of the differences between governments by the mass killing of peoples.

Today, as we move against the terrible scourge of war—as we go forward toward the greatest contribution that any generation of human beings can make in this world—the contribution of lasting peace, I ask you to keep up your faith. I measure the sound, solid achievement that can be made at this time by the straight edge of your own confidence and your resolve. And to you, and to all Americans who dedicate themselves with us to the making of an abiding peace, I say:

The only limit to our realization of tomorrow will be our doubts of today. Let us move forward with strong and active faith.

Index